Jay Amos Barrett

Evolution Of The Ordinance of 1787

With An Account Of The Earlier Plans For The Government Of The

Northwest Territory

Jay Amos Barrett

Evolution Of The Ordinance of 1787
With An Account Of The Earlier Plans For The Government Of The Northwest Territory

ISBN/EAN: 9783744653404

Printed in Europe, USA, Canada, Australia, Japan

Cover: Foto ©ninafisch / pixelio.de

More available books at **www.hansebooks.com**

UNIVERSITY OF NEBRASKA

DEPARTMENTS OF HISTORY
AND ECONOMICS

SEMINARY PAPERS

EVOLUTION

OF THE

ORDINANCE OF 1787

WITH AN ACCOUNT OF THE EARLIER PLANS FOR THE
GOVERNMENT OF THE NORTHWEST TERRITORY

BY

JAY A. BARRETT, M.A.

APRIL, 1891

G. P. PUTNAM'S SONS

NEW YORK   LONDON
27 WEST TWENTY-THIRD ST.   27 KING WILLIAM ST., STRAND

The Knickerbocker Press

1891

PRICE ONE DOLLAR

Departments of History and Economics.

George E. **Howard**, M.A., Professor of History.

Howard W. **Caldwell**, Ph.B., Associate Professor of History.

Amos G. **Warner**, Ph.D., Associate Professor of Economics and Political Science.

COURSES OF STUDY.

I. HISTORY.

(1) Ancient History: Epochs of Grecian and Roman History; Lectures on Athenian and Roman Institutions. Whole year, four hours.

(2) The Early Empire: General History of Civilization, with a special study of Roman Provincial Administration. First term, four hours.

(3) The Middle Ages: Selected Topics. Second and third terms, four hours.

(4) The Renaissance: Revival of Literature, Learning, Art, Politics, and Religion. First term, four hours.

(5) European History, 1500-1800: Protestant Revolution, Thirty Years' War, Puritan Revolution, Age of Anne. Whole year, three hours.

(6) The French Revolution. Second and third terms, three hours.

(7) Ancient Law: A Study of the Genesis of Aryan Institutions and of the History of Roman Law. First term, three hours.

(8) Growth of the English Constitution. Whole year, five hours.

(9) Political History of the Nineteenth Century. First term, three hours.

(10) American History to 1787. Whole year, five hours.

(11) American History: Formation of the Constitution; Ratification; Political and Constitutional Development to the Civil War; Reconstruction. Whole year, five hours.

II. ECONOMICS AND POLITICAL SCIENCE.

(1) Political Economy: General study of the subject with the use of some text. Lectures on the Character and History of the Science. Topical reports from students required, and exercises assigned in the use of statistics. First and second terms, three hours.

(2) Taxation: Text and lectures. Third term, three hours.

(3) International Law: Outline study of the subject, with text. Third term, three hours.

(4) Municipal Administration: Comparative study of the City Governments of the present time, with especial reference to American practice in the administrative branches. First and second terms, two hours.

(5) Constitutional Law. Third term, three hours.

(6) Private Corporations: First term, a comparative and historical view of corporation law in its economic aspects; second term, Railroad Problems; third term, special reports on assigned topics involving original research. Whole year, two hours.

(7) Charities and Corrections. Third term, three hours.

(8) Methods of Legislating: A comparative view of the rules and practice of modern legislative assemblies. First term, one hour.

III. SEMINARY OF HISTORY AND ECONOMICS.

Graduates, advanced undergraduates, and instructors in the two departments form an association for seminary work. Stated meetings are held for the presentation and discussion of papers and reports. Studies are made of economic and similar questions, based largely on corporation records, State archives, personal interviews, and correspondence. Other material for independent research is afforded by the libraries of the University, State, City, and Historical Society.

UNIVERSITY OF NEBRASKA

**DEPARTMENTS OF HISTORY
AND ECONOMICS**

SEMINARY PAPERS

EVOLUTION

OF THE

ORDINANCE OF 1787

WITH AN ACCOUNT OF THE EARLIER PLANS FOR THE
GOVERNMENT OF THE NORTHWEST TERRITORY

BY

JAY A. BARRETT, M.A.

APRIL, 1891

G. P. PUTNAM'S SONS

NEW YORK   LONDON
27 WEST TWENTY-THIRD ST.   27 KING WILLIAM ST., STRAND

The Knickerbocker Press

1891

PRICE ONE DOLLAR

The Knickerbocker Press, New York
Electrotyped, Printed, and Bound by
G. P. Putnam's Sons

EDITORIAL NOTE.

The starting of a new academic series ought to require no apology. On the contrary, it is a sign of progress that American universities are at last becoming centres of organized literary work. It can scarcely be doubted that the present decade, which has seen so much activity in this direction, will mark an important epoch in the history of American thought. Clearly, we have just reached a stage in higher educational development which has long since been entered upon by the schools of Germany. The ascendency of that nation in nearly every branch of science is mainly due to the fact that her scientific literature has its roots in the Seminar, which is at once the nursery and the workshop of the professorial body. Indeed German authorship as a whole is in no small measure the product of university specialization.

But it is not merely as an incentive or as a medium for the highest scholastic effort that such publication should be encouraged. There is much useful work which can be well done even by the young scholar of the graduate school. This is especially true in the various departments of economic and historical science. The statesmanship of the immediate future must concern itself largely with administrative problems ; and much of the material upon which wise action must rest has yet to be gathered. By aiding in the collection and publication of this material an important service to the State may be rendered by the school of political science.

Already much good work has been done. Is it not possible, however, that the efficiency of scientific study may be increased by a judicious division of labor? Some degree of differentiation according to locality or special opportunity would seem to be desirable. It will therefore be the aim of the *Seminary Papers*, while not excluding other topics, to deal mainly with questions relating to Western history and economics. Subsequent numbers will be issued from time to time as it may be found expedient.

CONTENT

EVOLUTION OF THE ORDINANCE OF 1787.

EVOLUTION OF THE ORDINANCE OF 1787.

I.

INTRODUCTION.

The Confederacy was a failure as a system of government, and its defects are too well known to need treatment here, except when they have an important bearing on the organization of unsettled lands. The conditions, however, under which the first plans were directly or indirectly developed arose mainly from the peculiar nature of that league between the States. The degree to which the Continental Congress was able to raise funds manifestly affected each branch of the administration and all kinds of laws. The inadequacy of the powers of that body had been felt from the first; but its actual helplessness was not realized until the close of the war, when the accumulated debt found less and less prospect of immediate liquidation and the army clamored loudest. When the true situation began to be seen, still greater questions presented themselves for solution. Congress must find some remedy for the financial distress of the impoverished country. It must feel its way blindly along the dim path of implied powers or trespass on the field of unconstitutionality, in order to care for a great West of which not only the resources and possibilities, but even the very limits, were vague in the minds of those best informed. Thus in the darkest hour of the Confederacy plans had begun to mature both for a better union of the existing States into a nation, and for the organization of the unoccupied territory; and before the national Constitution was ready, the Ordinance of 1787 had become a law. The latter was framed, therefore, during the so-called critical period of American history, and by the authority of the old Confederate Congress.

The claims of various States to vast tracts of western land under charters and conquests, and the cession of them to the central authority, are subjects not requiring present consideration. But it is in point here to mention the action connected with the adjustment of these supposed rights as contemporary with the first plans for western government and as determining in no small degree the attitude of Congress toward the region in question. No system of organization applying to this newly acquired domain could be seriously entertained until that assembly was acknowledged to have the right to legislate regarding it ; yet such plans began to develop while the States still looked fondly upon vast stretches of country and thought to realize prosperity therefrom. Attempts of States to retain something of that which they were asked to relinquish and limitation of the central power due to an imperfect title, were constant factors in shaping legislation touching disputed territory, as were also the condition of the army and that of the Treasury.

The western country began to be looked upon as a possible source of revenue very early in the war.[1] Indeed, as

[1] The attention of Congress was called to this idea in 1776 by Silas Deane. Writing from Paris, December 1, 1776, in a report to the Secret Committee, he spoke of the fertile tract of country between the Ohio, Mississippi, and Lakes as amply adequate to defray the whole expenses of the war, if properly managed : *American Archives,* Fifth Series, iii., 1020–1 ; Adams, *Maryland's Influence upon Land Cessions,* 22, citing Sparks, *Diplomatic Correspondence,* i., 79.   Mr. Deane also mentioned the idea to John Jay in a letter dated two days after his communication to Congress, in these words : "The western lands ought to be held up to view as an encouragement for our soldiers, especially foreigners, and are a good fund to raise money on" : *American Archives,* Fifth Series, iii., 1051. From this time forward frequent mention of the trans-Alleghany country as a prospective resource occurs in the correspondence of the time and in the records of Congress. "The other [*i.e.*, the cession of Virginia] will contribute to our funds," wrote Washington to Duane, February 19, 1781 : Bancroft, *Hist. of Formation of Const.,* i., 284–5.   The report of a grand committee on the subject, September 5, 1782, declares the opinion "that the western lands, if ceded to the United States, might contribute toward a fund for paying the

early as 1776 we find not only mention of this "fund to raise money on," but that Congress promises the soldiers bounties out of the land, and there are bold suggestions that it be parcelled out into independent States.[1] However, comparatively little attention was given to the financial possibilities of the unexplored wilderness until the end of the war. The idea more and more obtained that the public debt might be paid in whole or in part out of receipts from purchased lands. This prospect greatly aided those congressional measures which had for their object accession of title to the new region, as well as those which contemplated its organization.

debts of the states " : *Life of Cutler*, i., 129. *Cf.* another report, April 5, 1784 : *Ibid.* Congress had already taken advantage of the western lands before Mr. Deane made his suggestion, in offering bounties to soldiers. Acts of Congress to this effect bear the dates August 27 and September 16, 1776. Four years later another resolve was passed referring to the same subject (August 12, 1780). See on this, *American Archives*, Fifth Series, iii., 53, 120, 209, 211, 508–9, 788, 827, 1020–1, 1051, etc. ; *Life of Cutler*, i., 122.

[1] By Maryland in convention, November 9, 1776 : *American Archives*, Fifth Series, iii., 178.

II.

THE FIRST PLANS.

There were various reasons for the unusual attention paid to the western country in the spring of 1783. International arbitration gave excellent prospect for peace: in the preceding November provisional articles had been signed at Paris, a cessation of hostilities was declared in January, and there was every reason to expect a speedy close of the war. Peace meant the disbanding of the army, which would necessitate payment to the soldiers of at least enough money to enable them to reach home. Congress was thus forced to meet new demands upon the Treasury, and the eyes of its members were turned to the new lands, as a possible substitute for the long unpaid dues of the army. On the other hand, the soldiers were thoroughly dissatisfied with the complete failure of the government to supply their needs. In December, 1782, a number of officers petitioned Congress in behalf of the army.[1] Its inability to give definite answer led to bitter discontent, and finally resulted in the " Newburg Addresses " of March, 1783,[2] and the Philadelphia mutiny of the following June.[3] There were thus two motives for immediate action : the needs of the army on the one hand, and of the government on the other. The former produced the first results.

[1] The petition is printed in *Life of Cutler*, i., 152-4, taken from *Journals of Congress*, iv., 206.
[2] Pickering, *Life of Pickering*, i., 406 ff. ; Sparks, *Writings of Washington*, viii., 551-66.
[3] Pickering, *Life of Pickering*. i.. 474-5.

(a)— *The Army Plan.*

A scheme supported by some of the principal officers [1] originated about the first of April, 1783, and contemplated rewarding the soldiers with land in place of money. One of the principal movers was Pickering, in whose handwriting has been preserved a rough draft [2] of the propositions made. It was the work of several, among whom were also Huntington and Putnam. They intended to submit it first to the army, in order to learn the wishes of the soldiers, and to apply to Congress for the grant when all should be ready. How far it progressed or what became of it does not appear. Great interest was manifested, especially by Putnam, whose zeal in the cause is mentioned by Pickering in a letter of April 14, 1783.[3] But the policy of Congress was to obtain the territory by cession before venturing to organize it, and doubtless it was seen to be impracticable to urge the matter at that time. ' The plan bore the title, "*Propositions for settling a new State by such officers of the Federal Army as shall associate for that purpose.*" These propositions were as follows : (1) Purchase from the natives of a certain tract of country, the limits of which correspond to the present boundaries of Ohio. (2) Fulfilment of promises made to officers and soldiers by Congress in resolutions dating September 16, 1776, and August 13, and September 30, 1780. (3)–(6) Additional quantities of land for actual settlement by associators within one year after

---

[1] Timothy Pickering to Hodgdon, April 7, 1783 : " But a new plan is in contemplation—no less than forming a *new State* westward of the Ohio. Some of the principal officers of the army are heartily engaged in it. About a week since, the matter was set on foot, and a plan is digesting for the purpose. Enclosed is a rough draft of some propositions respecting it, which are generally approved of. They are in the hands of General Huntington and General Putnam for consideration, amendment, and addition. . . . As soon as the plan is well digested, it is intended to lay it before an assembly of the officers, and to learn the inclinations of the soldiers. If it takes, an application will then be made to Congress for the grant and all things depending on *them* " : Pickering, *Life of Pickering*, i., 457.

[2] Printed in Pickering, *Life of Pickering*, i., 546–9, Appendix iii.

[3] Pickering to Hodgdon, April 14, 1783 : *Ibid.*, i., 461.

purchase. (7) The formation of a common property of the
State from the surplus land, to be " disposed of for the
common good ; as for laying out roads, building bridges,
erecting public buildings, establishing schools and acade-
mies, defraying the expenses of government and other
public uses." (8) Clearing of a certain number of acres
within a specified time and erection of a house. (9) Equipment of associators by the government and payment by the
same of expenses in marching to place of settlement ;
equipment should include necessary utensils of husbandry,
live stock, and subsistence for three years. But cost of all
equipment should be charged to arrearages due associators.
(10) Equipment should also comprise arms and ammunition.
(11) Formation of a constitution for the new State by
associators before commencing settlement ; "the total exclusion of slavery from the State to form an essential and
irrevocable part." (12) Enactment of laws against crime
and for the preservation of the peace, to be in force two
years unless sooner repealed by an assembly of the State.
(13) Immediate admission of the prospective State into the
Union. (14) Election of delegates by associators, to take
their places as soon as the new State should be formed.
(15) Care by the State of families of disabled and deceased
associators.

Such was one of the very first [1] efforts to erect the frame-
work of a new republic out of the territory then just beginning to be occupied by settlers from all the Atlantic States.
The idea was that the State should be made up of men used
to military life ; and that, while justice would thus be done
the soldiers, they in turn would serve the Union by protect-
ing the frontiers. The need of the army, however, was the
occasion of this scheme. Its object was to obtain from the
government the dues of the army ; and these seemed to be

---

[1] Thomas Paine, in *Public Good*, 1780, also suggested a plan. This pam-
phlet announced on the title-page : " an investigation of the claims of Virginia
to the vacant western territory, and of the right of the United States to the
same ; with some outlines of a plan for laying out a new State, . . ." : Adams,
Maryland's Influence, 10, citing *Works of Thomas Paine*, i., 267. *Cf.* Winsor, *Narr. and Crit. Hist. of Amer.*, vii., 527–8.

forthcoming in no other form. Had this plan been carried out, the resulting State would probably have proved much more of a success from the stand-point of the associators, than from that of Congress. Its main constitutional features would have been drawn by men quite competent to the task. With the provisions for public improvements, and with the untempered anti-slavery proposition, the new State would have rid itself quickly of its peculiar relation to Congress, and ere long would have rivalled the older commonwealths in prosperity and thrift.

(b)—*The Financiers' Plan.*

In April, 1783, Washington wrote a long letter to Theodoric Bland in answer to some inquiries, stating the situation of the army at some length and requesting him to communicate the contents to Hamilton.[1] A few days later John Armstrong wrote to Washington, requesting him to drop a hint to Congress in regard to the subject named in the letter, viz., a plan for settling the western country.[2] Whatever may have been said by Washington relative to the subject, at any rate on June 5, Bland, supported by Hamilton, moved the adoption of an ordinance which was referred

---

[1] April 4, 1783, Bancroft : *Hist. of Formation of Const.,* i., 302-7.

[2] April 22, 1783 : *Ibid.,* 308. " The highest matter of national concern, in my opinion, is the preservation and regular settlement of the western country. That country, in a certain ratio, is equally the property of every state in the Union, and, if properly guarded from avaricious claimants and vagrants, may, at a very moderate price in the process of time, be sold out to a large amount indeed. It is also, under proper government, a solid fund for the security or discharge of national debt, and good titles there must induce the emigration of men of character and wealth from foreign parts. A proper republican plan for this great purpose is not very easily laid, but neither the plan nor the execution of it, I hope, will be thought impracticable. If that country is settled or taken up in an irregular and loose manner, these states will sustain an unknown loss, and the regular establishment of government will be greatly impeded, or, perhaps, something worse. I cannot consider that country in the same light we used to do other back lands clearly belonging to individual states ; it is the price of united blood and treasure, and ought neither to be partially engrossed, neglected, nor lavished away. Should these thoughts happen to concur with yours, an early hint to Congress may call this matter into contemplation."

to a grand committee.[1] But the question of the Virginia
cession was unsettled, and until this was determined, it was
thought best not to take action upon the ordinance.   This
document is in Mr. Bland's handwriting[2]; but it can scarcely
be his own production since others knew of it.   Possibly
Hamilton suggested some ideas.   The circumstances make
it probable that the occasion for it was the difficulty of the
Treasury in meeting the payments due the soldiers, rather
than any interest in their welfare or in the western country.
The plan of Pickering had been made from the stand-point
of the army; this one looked at the matter from the position of a financier.['] When the soldiers contemplated a settlement, they themselves intended to frame its constitution;
they proposed to be paid in full by Congress, not in paper
money, but in the necessaries of life; and they desired that
their colony should rank as a State from the first.['] The
character of the organization would affect them most of
all; and therefore there should be just laws, no slave should
be seen, and the State should be the guardian of widows
and orphans.   Such ideas are not found in the ordinance
offered by Mr. Bland, which appears in the character of
a financial measure intended to relieve the Confederation
from the pressure of debt.   The motion provided first for
the acceptance of the Virginia cession of 1781, without
guaranteeing to that State the territory which she had

[1] The time when Bland made the motion is in doubt, since the endorsement
on the original draft gives July 5, while the language used in the *Journals*,
under date of July 4, seems to indicate that the motion of Bland which contained the ordinance, was the same as the one on which a committee reported
July 4.   *Cf.* Bancroft, *Hist. of Formation of Const.*, i., 312, and Merriam,
Hist. of Ordinance, 7.   Merriam gives an extract from the *Journals*, July 4,
citing *Journals of Congress*, iv., 226–7.   Also Bancroft: *Hist. of Formation
of Const.*, i., 107, and *Hist. of U. S.* (Fin. Rev.), vi., 81; Winsor: *Narr. and
Crit. Hist. of Amer.*, vii., 528; *Ohio Arch. and Hist. Quar.*, ii., 79.   Mr.
Hinsdale is evidently in error when he states that this committee reported June
9: *Old Northwest*, 239.   Under this date Madison has: "Not states enough
assembled to form a Congress"; Elliot's *Debates*, v., 91.   Under date of July
5 Madison merely refers to the *Journals*.

[2] For the whole, see Bancroft, *Hist. of Formation of Const.*, i., 312–4.   *Cf.*
Merriam, *Hist. of Ordinance*, 6–7.

reserved south of the Ohio River ; and stated further, that in case Virginia agreed to these terms the ordinance should take effect on acceptance by the army.

The following are the main provisions : (1) Lands should be substituted in place of all commutation for half pay and arrearages due the army—thirty acres for every dollar due. This did not include the promised bounty lands. Furthermore, the land was to be free from taxation seven years. (2) There should be set apart for this purpose a tract of vacant territory lying within the bounds described in the preliminary treaty between the United States and Great Britain. (3) The territory so set apart should be laid off in districts not more than two degrees in latitude and three in longitude ; and each district should be divided into townships, the surveying to be done at the expense of the general government. (4) Any district should become a State and be admitted into the Union on an equality with the original States as soon as it contained twenty thousand male inhabitants. (5) Ten thousand out of every hundred thousand acres should be reserved as a domain for the use of the United States ; "the rents, shares, profits, and produce of which lands, when any such shall arise, to be appropriated to the payment of the civil list of the United States, the erecting frontier forts, the founding of seminaries of learning, and the surplus after such purposes (if any) to be appropriated to the building and equipping a navy, and to no other use or purpose whatever."

The scheme failed of success, because it was not yet clearly within the province of the general government to deal with the unoccupied territory. In their cause and purpose the two plans, it has been said, are very different. No less so are they in the boundaries proposed. Obviously a scheme involving land for the whole army must be more comprehensive than one where only " associators " were affected.

III.

Not at all satisfied with this state of affairs and determined
to make further efforts to move Congress regarding the
western lands, many officers of the Continental line petitioned for a new government in the unsettled country.
The prime mover among the 285 signers seems to have
been Rufus Putnam,[1] who was active in furthering the
former plan of the soldiers. This paper, dated June 16,
recites the resolves of Congress touching land grants, and
mentions the territory corresponding to the present State
of Ohio, as being "a tract of country not claimed as the
property of or in the jurisdiction of any particular state in
the Union,"[2] and proper for Congress to mark out into
a "distinct Government (or Colony of the United States) in
time to be admitted one of the confederate states of America." They asked further that when Congress had procured
the tract from the natives, the lands to which the petitioners were entitled should be located and surveyed and
provision made for all other officers and soldiers wishing

---

[1] Letter of Rufus Putnam to Washington, New Winsor, June 16, 1783, accompanying the petition : " The part which I have taken in promoting the petition
is well known, and therefore needs no apology, when I inform you that the signers expect that I will pursue measures to have it laid before Congress " : *Life of
Cutler*, i., 167. The petition is found in *Life of Cutler*, i., 159–167 ; *Ohio Arch.
and Hist. Quar.*, i., 38–46, with summary of the number of petitioners from each
State as follows : Massachusetts, 155 ; New Hampshire, 34 ; Connecticut, 46 ;
New Jersey, 36 ; Maryland, 13 ; New York, 1. *Cf.* also Bancroft, *Hist. of
Formation of Const.*, i., 314-5.

[2] *Life of Cutler*, i., 159.

to settle with them.   In regard to the ownership of the tract the petitioners had been misinformed ; and Washington, to whom the petition was sent in order that it might go to Congress with the weight of his approval, took care to remark in his accompanying letter that he did not pretend to say how far the tract of country mentioned in the petition was free from State claims.[1]   With the petition was a long letter from Putnam to Washington,[2] wherein he discussed the various questions connected with the project—such as the policy to be pursued regarding the natives and the commercial interests of the West.   But the most interesting part is that in which he writes of the accommodation that the land will afford the soldiers,[3] and of the local divisions proposed for the tract.[4]   He shows that they

---

[1] Washington to Pres. of Congress, June 17, 1783 : *Life of Cutler*, i., 172–4 ; Bancroft, *Hist. of Formation of Const.*, i., 315–17.

[2] Printed in *Life of Cutler*, i., 167–72.

[3] " The whole tract is supposed to contain about 17,418,240 acres, and will admit of 756 townships of six miles square, allowing to each township 3,040 acres for the ministry, schools, waste lands, rivers, ponds, and highways ; then each township will contain of settlers' lands 20,000 acres, and in the whole 15,120,000 acres.   The lands to which the army is entitled by the resolves of Congress referred to in the petition, according to my estimate, will amount to 2,106,850 acres, which is about the eighth part of the whole ; for the survey of this they expect to be at no expense, nor do they expect to be under any obligation to settle these lands, or do any duty to secure their title to them ; but in order to induce the army to become settlers in the new government, the petitioners hope Congress will make a further grant of lands on condition of settlement " : *Life of Cutler*, i., 171.

[4] " That the petitioners, at least some of them, are much opposed to the monopoly of lands, and wish to guard against large patents being granted to individuals, as in their opinion such a mode is very injurious to a country, and greatly retards its settlement, and whenever such patents are tenanted, it throws too much power into the hands of a few.   For these and many other obvious reasons the petitioners hope that no grants will be made but by townships of six miles square, or six by twelve, or six by eighteen miles, to be subdivided by the proprietors into six miles square, that being the standard on which they wish all calculations may be made, and that officers and soldiers as well as those who petition for charter on purchase, may form their associations on one uniform principle, as to number of persons or rights to be contained in a township, with the exception only that, when the grant is made for reward of services already done, or on condition of settlement, if the officers petition with the soldiers for a particular township, the soldiers shall have one right only to a captain's three, and so in proportion with commissioned officers of every grade " : *Ibid.*, 171-2.

intended to have townships of six[1] miles square; that the
question of setting apart lands in each township for education and the ministry was already well settled among
them; and that they expected the government to do the
surveying and give clear titles for grants already made.
The plan of April doubtless proved untimely. The army
now tried petition for the same purpose and prompted by
the same motive. Washington sent the two papers to Congress and endorsed the idea as " the most rational and prac-
ticable scheme which can be adopted by a great proportion
of the officers and soldiers of our army."[2] Thus were these
propositions brought to the notice of the Federal Assembly,
some of them new, some already much discussed. The time
of application could hardly have been more unfavorable.
The representatives gathered at Philadelphia were having an
experience not at all conducive to calm deliberations. On
June 21, the well-known mutiny of the Pennsylvania
soldiers took place, in which they besieged Congress in
its own hall.[3] On June 26[4] that body removed to Princeton, and the petitioners obtained no immediate results. It
is not difficult to see, however, that this paper, with the letters of Washington and Putnam, had not a little to do with

[1] Townships of this size were suggested in Congress at least as early as May 1,
1782, and November 3, 1781 : *Life of Cutler*, i., 337 ; Merriam, *Hist. of Ordinance*, 5. In an appendix to Smith's account of Bouquet's Expedition, the authorship of which is thought to belong to Thomas Hutchins, are expressed many of
the ideas which occur in the petition of June 16, 1783, and the letter of Putnam.
This appendix was published in 1765, and in it was the first announcement of
the " section " or square mile : Col. Charles Whittlesey, *Origin of the American
System of Land Surveys*, in *Miscellaneous Papers*, No. 15, p. 3.

[2] Washington to President of Congress, June 17, 1783 : *Life of Cutler*, i.,
174.

[3] Madison's account in Elliot's *Debates*, v., 92-4 ; McMaster, *Hist. of People
of U. S.*, i., 183-4 ; Pickering, *Life of Pickering*, i., 474-5 ; Marshall, *Life of
Washington*, iv., 615 ; Sparks, *Writings of Washington*, viii., 454-8 ; Cur-
tis, *Hist. of Const. of U. S.*, i., 219, note, and 220, note ; Hamilton to Reed,
Works of Hamilton, i., 374-5 ; Staples, *R. I. in Continental Congress*, 490 ;
Hamilton, *Hist. of Republic of U. S.*, ii., 560-8.

[4] Theo. Bland to Governor Harrison, July 5, 1783 : *Cal. Va. State Papers*, iii.
508. But *cf.* Madison in Elliot's *Debates*, v., 94 ; Hamilton, *Hist. of Republic
of U. S.*, ii., 564.

the discussions upon the subject of western lands after the removal.[1]

On the whole, the West, with its call for government and the conflict of claims upon it, occupied much of the time of the central authority. But action organizing or disposing of it was reserved until disputes were nearer settlement. The fruit of the summer's discussion began to appear when it was voted September 13, 1783, to accept the cession of Virginia without guaranteeing the territory not ceded.[2] Virginia modified her conditions, and October 20 empowered her delegates to make a cession.[3] The influence of the petition is more clearly seen in the proceedings of Congress on October 14, when Elbridge Gerry moved an amendment to the report of a committee on Indian affairs and western lands, embodying in his propositions[4] many of the ideas already advanced in Putnam's letter and the soldiers' request. More than half of the petitioners, 155 out of 285, were Massachusetts men. Gerry was one of their representatives in Congress, and naturally, therefore, was interested in promoting their cause.[5] The credit of the ideas advanced in Congress at this time concerning the West has been ascribed to the influence of Washington.[6] There were, indeed, on the same occasion other suggestions than those probably due to the petition of the soldiers and the letter of Putnam. One of these was that there be a period of territorial government before the establishment of a permanent constitution. Nothing in Washington's letter suggests this, and, furthermore, it appears to have been under discussion at Princeton during the summer.[7]

---

[1] This fact is learned from the correspondence of David Howell, of the following spring. Howell to Jonathan Arnold, February 21, 1784 : "The mode of government during the infancy of these States has taken up much time, and was largely debated at Princeton last summer " : *R. I. in Continental Congress*, 479.

[2] Donaldson, *Public Domain*, 67 ; Adams, *Maryland's Influence*, 38-9 ; Henning, *Statutes*, xi., 567-70.

[3] Henning, *Statutes*, xi., 326-8.

[4] *Life of Cutler*, i., 337-8 ; Merriam, *Hist. of Ordinance*, 7-8, giving October 15 instead of October 14, and citing *Journals of Congress*, iv., 296.

[5] *Cf. Life of Cutler*, i., 339.

[6] Adams, *Maryland's Influence*, 43.

[7] *R. I. in Continental Congress*, 479. In this connection it is well to notice,

The way to satisfy the claims of the soldiers and organize the West was evidently becoming clear. The deed of cession was not executed until March 1, 1784,[1] and by that time another ordinance had been prepared.

---

also, the statement that "the first definite plan for the formation of new States in the West, is to be found in a letter written the seventh of September, 1783, by General Washington to James Duane, Member of Congress from New York": Adams, *Maryland's Influence*, 41 ; Sparks, *Writings of Washington*, viii., 477–84. But as it has already appeared, the army plan of the spring and the petition of the summer had previously defined the boundaries of a proposed State. The project of Mr. Bland, also, although not stating clearly what should be the limits of the whole territory included, was really more comprehensive than the other two, since it would have organized sufficient territory for several States. Washington did, indeed, observe in the letter to Duane, that the country corresponding to the southern peninsula of the present State of Michigan would make a compact State ; but he was very far from being the first to point out a definite plan for dividing the West into States. Shosuke Sato has here followed Dr. Adams : *Land Question in U. S.*, 80–81.

[1] Winsor, *Narr. and Crit. Hist. of Amer.*, vii., 528, citing *Journals of Congress*, iv., 267, 342. Printed in Henning, *Statutes*, xi., 571–5 ; Donaldson, *Public Domain*, 68–69, etc.

I.

PROPOSED DIVISION OF THE WEST IN THE
PLAN OF MARCH 1, 1784.

IV.

THE LAW OF 1784.

BIBLIOGRAPHICAL NOTE.—Dunn, *Indiana*, 180–8 ; Peter Force, *Hist. of Ordinance*, in *St. Clair Papers*, ii., 603–6, and *Life of Cutler*, ii., 407–11 ; Randall, *Life of Jefferson*, i., 397–400 ; Sato, *Land Question in the U. S.*, 80–6 ; Bancroft, *Hist. of U. S.* (Fin. Rev.), vi., 116–8, and *Hist. of Formation of Const.*, i., 356–7, 367 ; Winsor, *Narr. and Crit. Hist. of Amer.*, vii., 528 ; Donaldson, *Public Domain*, 146–9 ; Stone, *The Ordinance of 1787*, in *Penn. Mag. of Hist. and Biog.*, xiii., 313–4, 320, 327 ; Curtis, *Hist. of the Const.*, i., 296–9 ; ii., 343, 345–6 ; *Life of Cutler*, i., 338, 362–3 ; Walker, *Hist. of Athens County, O.*, 40 ; McMaster, *Hist. of People of U. S.*, i., 165–7, citing *New York Tribune*, Dec. 30, 1856, and *Tribune Almanac*, 1857 ; Dillon, *Hist. of Indiana*, 182 ; Adams, *Maryland's Influence*, 42, 44–5, 47, and *Nation*, xxxiv., 384 (May 4, 1882) ; King, *Ohio*, 178–9 ; *Ohio Arch. and Hist. Quar.*, i., 5, 7, 12, 22, 32 ; ii., 37, 46, 79, 80 ; Hinsdale, *Old Northwest*, 266, 269, 273–4, and *Mag. of West. Hist.*, vi., 267 ; Sparks, *Writings of Washington*, ix., 47–8 ; Poole, *No. Am. Rev.*, vol. cxxii., No. 251, pp. 237–9 (April, 1876) ; Davidson and Stuvé, *Hist. of Illinois*, 206–7 ; *Report of Commissioner of Centennial Celebration, Marietta, O.. 1888*, 147–8, 219 ; Morse, *Thomas Jefferson*, 75–6 ; Fiske, *Crit. Period of Amer. Hist.*, 196–9 ; Staples, *R. I. in the Cont. Cong.*, 478–81, 485, 494 ; Cooley, *Michigan*, 125–6 ; Hildreth, *Hist. of U. S.*, iii., 449–50 ; Pickering, *Life of Pickering*, i., 508–10 ; Perkins, *Annals of the West*, 292 ; Williams, *Hist. of Negro Slavery in Amer.*, i., 416 ; Porter, *Outlines of Const. of U. S.*, 62 ; Eliot, *Hist. of U. S.*, 274–5 ; Arnold, *Hist. of State of R. I.*, ii., 507 ; I. W. Andrews, in *Mag. of Amer. Hist.*, xvi., 136–7, 139 ; Cox, *Three Decades of Federal Legislation*, 42–3 ; Merriam, *Hist. of Ordinance*, 8–13 ; Knight, *Hist. of Land Grants for Education in N. W. Terr.*, 10, 15 ; Edwards, *Hist. of Illinois*, 7, 8 ; Johnston, *Ordinance of 1787*, in Lalor's *Cyclopædia of Pol. Sci.*, iii., 30–1 ; Taylor, *Hist. of Ohio*, 505–9 ; Von Holst, *Const. Hist. of U. S.*, *1750–1832*, 286–7 ; Mich. Pioneer and Hist. Coll., vii., 18 ; Moses, *Illinois, Historical and Statistical*, i., 184 ; Linn, *Life of Jefferson*, 142–3.

(a)—*Jefferson's Draft.*

On the day of the cession by the Virginia delegates a committee reported a plan for the temporary government of the western territory. Mr. Jefferson was chairman, the other members being Mr. Chase of Maryland, and **Mr.** Howell of Rhode Island. They had already agreed to their report as early as February 21, as appears from the correspondence of members of the committee.[1] The letters of Mr. Howell especially throw light upon the intentions of the committee, and make possible a more nearly correct construction of the report.

The plan[2] is very different in many respects from any thing previously suggested for the West. Except the introductory clause the first paragraph of the report is devoted to a scheme for dividing the country into States. That clause, however, is very significant. The territory which is to be divided, is that " ceded or to be ceded " by the individual States ; and the plan does not stop at the limits of the cession which the Virginia delegates completed on the day of the report. From parallel 31°, the northern boundary of the Spanish possessions, to the northern boundary of the United States as defined not long before in the treaty of peace, the odd parallels of latitude are to form north and south boundaries of States ; while two meridians, passing through the " lowest point of the rapids of the Ohio," and the "western cape of the mouth of the Great Kenawha," cut these tiers of States into three parts. The Mississippi forms the western boundary ; for it was not given to the Congress of the Confederation to discover undeveloped possibilities beyond that river. There were thus from north to south eight tiers of States. The real intention of the committee, however, did not appear in the report. It was their purpose to allow the middle section of States, which was bounded east and west by the two meridians, to reach no farther south than the northern boundary of South Car-

[1] Howell to Jonathan Arnold, February 21, 1784 : " The report is agreed to by the committee, but has not yet been made to Congress " : *R. I. in Continental Congress*, 479.

[2] It is in the handwriting of Jefferson, in the State Department, and is printed in Randall, *Life of Jefferson*, i., 397–9 ; Force, *Hist. of Ordinance*, in *St. Clair Papers*, ii., App. i., 603–5, and *Life of Cutler*, ii., 407–10 ; Merriam, *Hist. of Ordinance*, 8–10. In Donaldson, *Public Domain*, 147–8, part is omitted.

2

olina, in order that this State and Georgia might extend to
the more western meridian.¹ The territory between the
Kenawha meridian, the Ohio River, Pennsylvania, and Lake
Erie was to be one State. They assumed that Virginia and
North Carolina, also, would be bounded on the west by this
meridian, either by cession on their part or by action of
Congress. All territory north of latitude 47° was to belong
to the State immediately south, and that comprehended
within Lake Michigan, Lake Huron, and parallel 43°, was
intended to be one State. Carrying out the letter of the
plan, there were sixteen States outlined; but leaving out
the two States that would be formed by extending the part
between the meridians southward below the northern boundary of South Carolina, there were fourteen ² States. To

¹ A letter which is of much value in showing the first idea of the committee
about dividing the West, appears to have been thus far overlooked in the discussion of this question. It is one written by David Howell to Jonathan Arnold,
February 21, 1784, in which he said : " It is proposed to divide the country into
fourteen new states, in the following manner. There are to be three tiers of
states :—one on the Atlantic, one on the Mississippi, and a middle tier. The
middle tier is to be the smallest and to form a balance betwixt the two more
powerful ones. The western tier of states is to be bounded eastwardly by
a meridional line drawn through the lowest point of the rapids of the river Ohio,
and the eastern tier is to be bounded westwardly by a meridional line drawn
through the west cape of the mouth of the great ——— from Lake Erie to the
north boundary of South Carolina, where the middle tier of states ends, and
permits South Carolina and Georgia to run west to the first mentioned meridional line, as their Atlantic coast falls off west " : *R. I. in Continental Congress*,
479. Unless the committee intended to terminate the middle section of States
at the northern boundary of South Carolina, very little territory would remain to
Georgia, and South Carolina would be smaller than now. The construction
shown by the letter is, therefore, given in the text. Mention is often made of a
plan for seventeen States, but it seems to be incorrect by any construction. *Cf.*
McMaster, *Hist. of People of U. S.*, i., 165, and others. See Map I.

² Mr. Dunn errs somewhat in stating that " the original plan provided for the
formation of ten states, all in the territory northwest of the Ohio " : *Indiana*,
180. It will be seen, if traced out on a map, that only eight lie north of parallel 39°, and even this parallel cuts the north bend of the Ohio. In the original
draft no provision is made for the Ohio to be a boundary, except the one providing that so much of the point of land at the confluence of the Ohio and Mississippi as might lie south of parallel 37° should be included in the State lying
immediately north of it ; but there was no need for this one, since that parallel
does not cut the territory north of the Ohio. His supposition that " the origi-

ten of these, names [1] were given. The common statement that Jefferson would have divided the West into ten States may be attributed to the fact that only that number received names.

The districts do not differ much in size from those proposed by the ordinance of Mr. Bland, which were two degrees in latitude and three in longitude. A resolution of Congress on October 10, 1780, respecting cessions of the western territory, mentions States of "not less than one hundred nor more than one hundred and fifty miles square."[2] This had been repeated by Virginia in her acts

nal report provided only for the division of lands northwest of the Ohio and apparently was not intended to apply south of that stream, while the second report covered all the territory west of the Alleghanies" (*Indiana*, 181), seems also to be incorrect. The original report, or the one made March 1, 1784, states expressly that the division into States should begin "from the completion of thirty-one degrees north of the equator": Randall, *Life of Jefferson*, i., 397-8; Force, *Hist. of Ordinance*, in *St. Clair Papers*, ii., 603; Donaldson, *Public Domain*, 147. The second report, on the other hand, if it agreed in this particular with the ordinance as passed April 23, says that the new States shall comprehend *from north to south*, beginning to count from parallel 45°. The first report reads, "from south to north." The second says nothing about 31° or about States south of the Ohio River. The latter was rather more in harmony with the Virginia theory than the former. Indeed, there is evidence tending to show that Jefferson was not the exponent of the Virginia theory, in regard to the western country. In a letter to Madison, February 20, 1784, he writes : "We hope North Carolina will cede all beyond the same meridian of Kenawha, and Virginia also ": Bancroft, *Hist. of Formation of Const.*, i., 343. Washington in a letter to Jefferson dated March 29, 1784, understands Jefferson to think the same way, as he writes of the impolicy of Virginia's trying to retain more territory than she can govern, and adds : "for the reasons you assign, I very much approve of a meridian from the mouth of the Great Kenawha as a convenient and very proper line of separation, but I am mistaken if our chief magistrate will coincide with us in this opinion ": Sparks, *Writings of Washington*, ix., 33. Mr. King, in *Ohio*, 178, shows a similar misconception with regard to the situation of these States.

[1] The names have been the cause of much amusement on the part of writers. They are : Sylvania, Michigania, Cheronesus, Metropotamia, Assenisipia, Illinoia, Saratoga, Washington, Polypotamia, and Pelisipia. *Cf.* Adams, *Maryland's Influence*, 42, 47 ; *Nation*, May 4, 1882 ; Morse, *Jefferson*, 75-6 ; Fiske, *Crit. Period of Amer. Hist.*, 196-8.

[2] Donaldson, *Public Domain*, 64 ; Winsor, *Narr. and Crit. Hist. of Amer.*, vii., 527, citing *Journals of Congress*, iii., 535 ; Sato, *Land Question*, 82 ; Adams, *Maryland's Influence*, 35 ; Merriam, *Hist. of Ordinance*, 4. Shosuke

and deed of cession.   A proposition offered May 1, 1782, would have enlarged the divisions to one hundred and thirty miles square.' But the resolution of 1780 is regarded in a report ' subsequent to the plan of 1784 as having determined the size of States outlined in that scheme.   No one of the proposed States was to be formed until the territory should be ceded to the United States, if not already ceded, and Congress should purchase the land of the Indian inhabitants and offer it for sale.   The part of the report specifying how the temporary government was to be formed, is as follows : " The settlers within the territory so to be purchased and offered for sale, shall, either on their own petition, or on the order of Congress, receive authority from them, with appointments of time and place for their free males, of full age, to meet together for the purpose of establishing a temporary government, to adopt the constitution and laws of any one of these states, so that such laws nevertheless shall be subject to alteration by their ordinary legislature ; and to erect, subject to a like alteration, counties or townships for the election of members for their legislature."   When any State acquired 20,000 free inhabitants,' it was to give proof of the fact to Congress and receive from that body " authority, with appointments of time and place, to call a convention of representatives to establish a permanent constitution and government for themselves."

The report contained, however, a statement of the following principles, along the line of which these new governments must move in their establishment and growth : (1) They shall for ever remain a part of the United States of

---

Sato thinks that " Mr. Jefferson must have been governed by the resolution of Congress, October 10, 1780," because the area of the northwestern cessions is estimated at 265,877.91 square miles, and the area of ten States, each being 150 miles square, amounts to 225,000 square miles : *Land Question*, 82–3.

¹ *Life of Cutler*, i., 337 ; Merriam. *Hist. of Ordinance*, 5, giving the report of the previous autumn, November 3, 1781, and taking it from *Papers of Old Congress*, vol. xxx.

² Bancroft, *Hist. of U. S.* (Fin. Rev.), vi., 278 ; Merriam, *Hist. of Ordinance*, 17.

³ *Cf.* " 20,000 male inhabitants " in Bland's ordinance : above, Sec. II., (b).

America; (2) they shall be subject to the government of Congress and the Articles of Confederation, and (3) shall be liable for their share of the Federal debts; (4) the government shall be republican, barring from citizenship any one holding an hereditary title; (5) and "after the year 1800 of the Christian era there shall be neither slavery nor involuntary servitude in any of the said states, otherwise than in punishment of crimes, whereof the party shall have been duly convicted to have been personally guilty." The last provision does not bear comparison with the proposal in the army plan about a year before, to exclude slavery forthwith from the prospective State. Probably Jefferson knew only too well the reception which an anti-slavery proposition would receive in Congress, and perhaps he thought that the one offered by the committee would receive more favor than an immediate prohibition. There is no reason to doubt the genuineness of Jefferson's anti-slavery views. He may have favored the extension of time which he reported, because the sentiment in Congress would not support stronger measures, or he may have had in view the fact that there were a few slaves in the western territory already. At any rate, this was the committee's decision; and no doubt it was difficult for them to realize the full meaning of the concession. They should have the credit of desiring to remove slavery from the whole West, but they were not alive to the possibilities of an undeveloped and, for the most part, unsettled country, ready to receive the effect of a pro-slavery or an anti-slavery constitution. Professor McMaster points to this provision of March 1, 1784, as "the first attempt at at a national condemnation of slavery."[1]

After gaining a population of twenty thousand, the inhabitants of a State might indeed form a permanent government with a constitution of their own; but this did not admit to the Confederacy. There was also a provision that " whensoever any of the states shall have, of free inhabitants, as many as shall then be in any one of the least numerous of the thirteen original states, such state shall be

---

[1] *Hist. of People of U. S.*, i., 167.

admitted by its delegates into the Congress of the United States, on an equal footing with the said original states." After the accession of one State, there was to be substituted a two-thirds vote of Congress in cases where the consent of nine States was before required[1]; but this was not meant to affect the vote for admission of States, as expressed in Article XI. of the Articles of Confederation.

Even during temporary government provision was made that the voice of the people might be heard in Congress. The State, while in this stage, might keep a member in Congress, who should have the right to speak but not to vote. The final paragraph deserves to be quoted in full, because of the part which the ideas therein expressed played in the later development of the territorial governments: "The preceding articles shall be formed into a Charter of Compact, shall be duly executed by the President of the United States in Congress assembled, under his hand and the seal of the United States, shall be promulgated, and shall stand as fundamental constitutions between the thirteen original states and those now newly described, unalterable but by the joint consent of the United States in Congress assembled, and of the particular state within which such alteration is to be made."

(b)—*The Second Report.*

The scheme was not satisfactory, and on March 17[2] it was referred to the same committee again to be revised. In a new report[3] nearly a week later, the part containing

---

[1] In the previous summer a motion had been made in Congress by Williamson, seconded by Bland, that whenever a fourteenth State should be added, a vote of ten States should be required where that of nine was sufficient before : Elliot, *Debates*, v., 92.

[2] Donaldson, *Public Domain*, 148 ; Peter Force, *Hist. of Ordinance*, in *St. Clair Papers*, ii., 605, and *Life of Cutler*, ii., 410. March 3 had been assigned for its consideration : Merriam, *Hist. of Ordinance*, 8.

[3] Most writers give the 22d of March for this : Donaldson, *Public Domain*, 148 ; Dunn, *Indiana*, 182 ; McMaster, *Hist. of the People of the U. S.*, i., 165 (where an error is made in stating that the second report contained the names of the States). But Mr. Merriam cites the endorsement upon the second report as : "Report on Western territory. Delivered March 23, 1784. Read,

the names was omitted, and the boundaries of some of the
States to be laid out north of the river were changed.[1]
Here, however, the division of the territory south of the
Ohio was merely implied. It made six entire States north
of the Ohio, besides the corner next to Pennsylvania and
Lake Erie, one third the size of the State now occupying
that position. The extreme northwest was left unorganized, because the measure did not apply above parallel 45°,
except between the meridians. It covered the land " ceded
or to be ceded," and there was prospect for half a dozen
more States south of the six that have been mentioned,
provided the land beyond the Alleghanies should be yielded
to the general government.

Wednesday 24th assigned for consideration " : *Hist. of Ordinance,* 10. The
error of Mr. Dunn has been noticed already. His idea appears to be that the
first report looked only to the division of the territory northwest of the Ohio
River ; that in so putting it, Jefferson was supporting the "Virginia theory" ;
that the real object in resubmitting the report was to provide for the land south
of the Ohio also. But Jefferson's personal endeavor from the start was to have
Virginia cede the lands from the Kenawha meridian, and both reports covered
the territory south of the Ohio as well as that north of it. Moreover the influence
of the rest of the committee should not be overlooked.

  [1] That the changes in boundaries were made by the committee before their
second report is inferred from the language of Mr. Dunn : *Indiana,* 181 ; but
cf. Randall, *Life of Jefferson,* i., 400. The principal alterations were : that
the territory "which may lie beyond the completion of the 45th degree,
between the said meridians, shall make part of the State adjoining it on the
south ; and that part of the Ohio, which is between the said meridians, coin-
ciding nearly with the parallel of 39 degrees, shall be substituted so far in lieu
of that parallel as a boundary line." But if only that part of the territory
north of parallel 45°, which lies "between the said meridians," was to be
added to the territory south of it, northern Wisconsin and northwestern Michigan, as they are to-day, were not included in the territory to be divided. For
the divisions were to begin at parallel 45°, counting "from north to south."
Writers generally give the ordinance of April 23, which passed with these
changes, as dividing the West into ten States. *Cf.* one of the latest, Merriam,
Hist. of the Ordinance, 12. It is even stated that there were to be ten States
all northwest of the Ohio. The number provided for by the second report
entirely on this side of the river is limited to seven. The estimates for the
whole West, south as well as north of the Ohio, necessarily vary with the
amount of unceded land taken into consideration. If everything west of the
Kenawha meridian is divided, there results fifteen States. If the same restriction which the committee first intended, is made, as to the part between the
meridians, and if the division is otherwise carried to parallel 31°, the plan gives
thirteen States. See Map II.

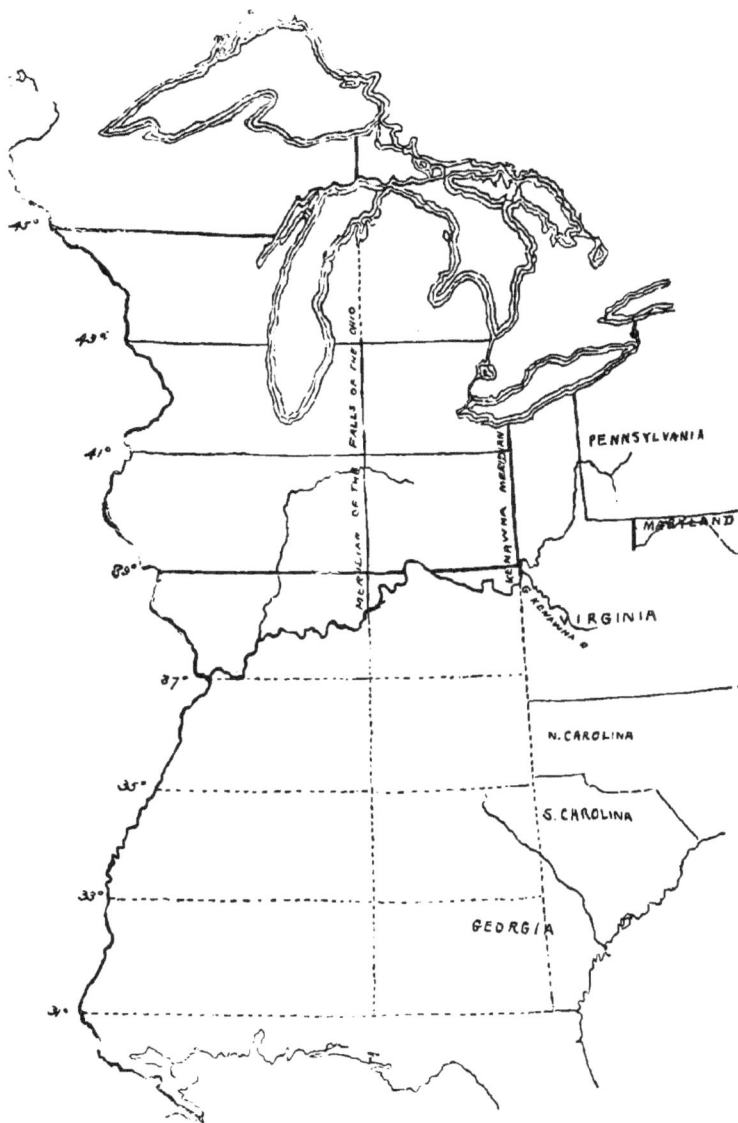

PENNSYLVANIA

MARYLAND

VIRGINIA

G. KENHAWA

N. CAROLINA

S. CAROLINA

GEORGIA

MERIDIAN OF THE FALLS OF THE OHIO

KENHAWA MERIDIAN

II.

DIVISION OF THE WEST IN THE ORDINANCE OF
APRIL 23, 1784.

In the consideration of the report by Congress, further
amendments were made, some of which touched the ordinance at vital points. On April 19 the proviso limiting
slavery was dropped. A North Carolina delegate ' moved
to have the clause struck out, and upon the question
whether it should stand or not, it failed to receive the
requisite number of votes. After further amendment dur-

---

[1] The motion was made by Richard D. Spaight, who came to Congress May
13, 1783 : Sparks, *Writings of Washington*, xii., 424. Upon the question,
"Shall the words moved to be struck out stand?" Mr. Howell required the
yeas and nays. The votes were as follows :

New Hampshire, *aye :* Abiel Foster and Jonathan Blanchard.

Massachusetts, *aye :* Elbridge Gerry and George Partridge.

Rhode Island, *aye :* William Ellery and David Howell.

Connecticut, *aye :* Roger Sherman and James Wadsworth.

New York, *aye :* Charles De Witt and Ephraim Paine.

New Jersey, — : Samuel Dick, *aye ;* John Beatty, absent.

Pennsylvania, *aye :* Thomas Mifflin, John Montgomery, and Edward Hand.

Maryland, *no :* James McHenry and Thomas Stone.

Virginia, *no :* Thomas Jefferson, *aye ;* Samuel Hardy, *no ;* John F. Mercer,
no ; James Monroe, absent.

North Carolina, — : Hugh Williamson, *aye ;* Richard D. Spaight, *no.*

South Carolina, *no :* Jacob Read and Richard Beresford.

Georgia, absent.

The vote of New Jersey could not be counted, since but one delegate was
present. Mr. Monroe would have voted with Mr. Jefferson, had he not been
absent on account of sickness, and thus would have prevented a negative vote
by Virginia : Jefferson to Madison, April 25, 1784, in Bancroft, *Hist. of Formation of Const.*, i., 356–8. Jefferson regretted the failure of the proposition
and the individual vote of Virginia in the negative ; but it must have been
apparent to others besides Pickering that "the admission of it (slavery) for a
day or an hour ought to have been forbidden" : Letter of Pickering to King,
March, 8, 1785, Pickering, *Life of Pickering*, i., 510. *Cf.* the following :
Randall, *Life of Jefferson*, i., 399–400, citing *Journals of Congress*, iv., 373
(Way and Gideon's Edition) ; Donaldson, *Public Domain*, 148 ; *St. Clair
Papers*, ii., 605 ; *Life of Cutler*, ii., 410–1 ; Dunn, *Indiana*, 184–5 ; King,
Ohio, 178–9 ; Sato, *Hist. of Land Question*, 84–5 ; McMaster, *Hist. of People
of U.S.*, 167 ; Dillon, *Hist. of Indiana*, 182 ; Bancroft, *Hist. of Formation
of Const.*, i., 156, and *Hist. of U. S.* (Fin. Rev.), vi., 117–8 ; *Ohio Arch. and
Hist. Quar.*, i., 12 ; ii., 37 ; Benton, *Thirty Years' View*, i., 133 ; Poole, *Dr.
Cutler and the Ordinance of 1787, No. Am. Review*, vol. 122, p. 238 ; *R. I.
in Continental Congress*, 494 ; Wilson, *Rise and Fall of Slave Power*, i., 32 ;
Williams, *Hist. of Negro Race in Amer.*, i., 416 ; *Works of Webster*, iii., 283 ;
Hinsdale, *Old Northwest*, 273 ; Stone, in *Penn. Mag. of Hist. and Biog.*,
xiii., 314 ; Merriam, *Hist. of Ordinance*, 10–12.

ing the next two days the ordinance was passed April 23, 1784, and became the law for the western territory.

Some of the other changes made in the ordinance before it passed were by no means unimportant. The clause against hereditary titles was omitted, and three new " principles " inserted. One denied the right of future States formed under the ordinance to " interfere with the primary disposal of the soil by the United States in Congress assembled," or " with the ordinances and regulations which Congress may find necessary for securing the title in such soil to the bona-fide purchasers." No lands belonging to the United States should be taxed, and non-resident owners of land in the prospective States should not be taxed higher than resident owners before the admission of their State to Congress by delegate.[1] A motion made by Mr. Read of South Carolina during the discussion of the ordinance is of more significance as pointing out the exact way in which the Federal government afterwards controlled the new territories, than for its effect upon the plan as passed. He proposed that " until such time as the settlers aforesaid shall have adopted the constitution and laws of some one of the original states as aforesaid for a temporary government, the said settlers shall be ruled by magistrates to be appointed by the United States in Congress assembled, and under such laws and regulations as the United States in Congress assembled shall direct." [2] This did not again find expression even as a report of a committee until two years later.

Such is the well-known " Ordinance of 1784," which, though inoperative, was legally in force until 1787. It has been characterized as " a compromise measure dictated by the general feeling in Congress," [3] but there is little or no ground for so designating it. Jefferson gives a possible reason for its receiving favor enough to be passed, in saying

---

[1] Compare the two drafts in Donaldson, 147–9 ; Merriam, 8–10 ; Force's *History*, in *St. Clair Papers*, ii., App. i., and *Life of Cutler*, ii., App. D. ; etc.

[2] *Life of Cutler*, i., 362–4 ; Merriam, *Hist. of Ordinance*, 12. '

[3] Dunn, *Indiana*, 184.

to Madison : " The act of Congress now enclosed to you will show you that they have agreed to it because it extends not only to the territory ceded but to be ceded, and shows how and when they shall be taken into the Union." [1]   On the whole, this attempt to legislate for the West was more successful than previous trials.   It did indeed become a law, but had little application to the region because systematic settlement could not be made. ⌐On this point Congress had not yet spoken, since the Indians possessed the lands.   The framers of this law were not so unwise as they might seem at first glance, for it was intended to enact, at the same time, a law to govern the disposal of the lands.   In this way immediate settlement would have begun.   Jefferson tells Madison in the letter just quoted that " the minuter circumstances of selling the ungranted lands will be pro-vided in an ordinance already prepared but not reported." [1] It was presented to Congress in due time, but for some reason was not favorably received. [3]   Without some such regulation the Ordinance of 1784 was a dead letter.

---

[1] April 25, 1784 : Bancroft, *Hist. of Formation of Const.*, i., 356.

[3] Bancroft, *Hist. of Formation of Const.*, i., 356.

[3] Jefferson was chairman of the committee who reported this ordinance for locating and disposing of the public lands, his associates being Williamson of North Carolina, Howell of Rhode Island, Gerry of Massachusetts, and Read of South Carolina.   Six States voted squarely against the report.   *Cf.* Randall, *Life of Jefferson*, i., 400 ; Merriam, *Hist. of Ordinance*, 13-14.

V.

THE REVIVAL OF THE SLAVERY PROVISO.

BIBLIOGRAPHICAL NOTE.—Dunn, *Indiana*, 190–4 ; Bancroft, *Hist. of U. S.* (Fin. Rev.), vi., 132–4, and *Hist. of Formation of Const.*, i., 178–80, 417–19 ; *Life of Cutler*, i., 353 ; *St. Clair Papers*, i., 123 ; Merriam, *Hist. of Ordinance*, 14–7 ; Force, *Hist. of Ordinance*, in *St. Clair Papers*, ii., 606–7, and *Life of Cutler*, ii., 411–2 ; Pickering, *Life of Pickering*, i., 504–11 ; Donaldson, *Public Domain*, 149–50 ; Curtis, *Hist. of Const.*, i., 299 ; IIinsdale, *Old Northwest*, 273–4 ; Stone, in *Penn. Mag. of IIist. and Biog.*, xiii., 314–5 ; Wilson, *Rise and Fall of Slave Power*, i., 32 ; McMaster, *Hist. of People of U. S.*, i., 253, Washington, *Writings of Jefferson*, ix., 276 ; *Journals of Congress*, iv., 481–2 ; *Papers of Old Congress*, xxxi.. 327, 329, 331 ; *Ohio Arch. and Hist. Quar.*, ii., 38.

Thus far the strongest proposition to restrict slavery from the West was contained in the first plan for a new State. While it cannot be asserted positively that Timothy Pickering was the author of this feature of it, his later course shows that it must have received his heartiest approval. Two years afterwards he appeared again as a strong opponent of slavery. Like many other soldiers, he was looking beyond the Alleghanies to settle. Just before the enactment of the well-known land ordinance of 1785, he became solicitous about the manner of locating claims in the new country, and thought that some system should be immediately provided. Elbridge Gerry was representing Massachusetts in Congress during 1784–5, and it was to him that Mr. Pickering wrote, March 1, 1785, in order to learn what the general government would do in the matter.[1] Mr. Gerry was at that time on the point of returning home, and therefore sent him a copy of a bill then before Congress, and referred him to the other Massachusetts representative,

---

[1] Pickering, *Life of Pickering*, i., 504–6.

Rufus King. This bill was a plan for locating and surveying lands, which later became a law. It has its own history
and in itself little concerns the acts for governing the West.
But in commenting upon it in a letter to King,[1] Mr.
Pickering took occasion to refer to the clause on slavery
erased by the previous Congress from Jefferson's draft.
Having mentioned the act of April 23, 1784, he wrote
further: "'There is one article in the report of the committee on which that act was made which I am extremely sorry
to see was omitted in the act. The committee proposed
that after the year 1800 there should be no slavery in the
new States. I hardly have the patience to write on a subject in which what is right is so obvious and so just, and
what is wrong is so derogatory to Americans above all men,
so inhuman and iniquitous in itself." He said much of excluding slavery from the unsettled country, and finally
appealed to him to make one more effort "to prevent so
terrible a calamity."[2]   Only eight days after the date of
Pickering's letters, Rufus King brought forward the following motion : " Resolved that there shall be neither slavery
nor involuntary servitude in any of the States described in
the resolve of Congress of the twenty-third day of April,
A.D. 1784, otherwise than in punishment of crimes whereof
the party shall have been personally guilty. And that this
regulation shall be an article of compact and remain a fun-

---

[1] Pickering, *Life of Pickering*, i., 506–10, two letters dated March 8, 1785.

[2] One of Pickering's statements has been objected to as inaccurate. He says :
" To suffer the continuance of slaves until they can gradually be emancipated in
states already over-run with them, may be pardonable, because unavoidable
without hazarding greater evils ; but to introduce them into countries where
none now exist—countries which have been talked of, which we have boasted of
as asylums to the oppressed of the earth—can never be forgiven."—Pickering,
Life of Pickering, i., 510.   To be sure, there was a handful of slave-holding
French in the small villages on the Wabash, Illinois, and Mississippi ; and who-
ever caused the slave-clause to be inserted in the draft of March 1, 1784, may
have been thinking also of the new settlements in the Kentucky and Tennessee
region.   Yet the country was practically unsettled, and the character of new
territories and States, as affected by the toleration or prohibition of slavery, was
still to be determined. *Cf.* Dunn, *Indiana*, 192, note 1 ; Stone, *Penn. Mag.
of Hist. and Biog.*, xiii., 327, note.

damental principle of the constitutions of the thirteen
original States, and each of the States described in
the said resolve of the twenty-third day of April, 1784." [1]
He moved that the proposition be committed, and upon
being carried [2] it was intrusted to Rufus King, David Howell,
and William Ellery.   Their report, which was presented by
Mr. King on April 26, differed in important points from
the motion committed.   It restored the lease of life to
slavery, and added the afterward famous fugitive-slave
clause.   The report of the committee was as follows : " Resolved that after the year 1800 of the Christian era there
shall be neither slavery nor involuntary servitude in any of
the states described in the resolve of Congress of the twenty-
third day of April, 1784, otherwise than in punishment of
crimes whereof the party shall have been personally guilty ;
and that this regulation shall be an article of compact, and
remain a fundamental principle of the Constitutions between
the thirteen original states and each of the states described
in the said resolve of Congress of the twenty-third day of
April, 1784, any implication or construction of the said
resolve to the contrary notwithstanding.   Provided always
upon the escape of any person into any of the states
described in the said resolve of Congress of the twenty-
third day of April, 1784, from whom labor or service is lawfully claimed in any one of the thirteen original states, such
fugitive may be lawfully reclaimed and carried back to the
person claiming his labor or service as aforesaid, this resolve
notwithstanding." [3]   It is evident from the resolutions of

---

[1] Donaldson, *Public Domain*, 149 ; Bancroft, *Hist. of Formation of Const.*,
i., 417, citing *Papers of Old Congress*, No. 31, p. 327 ; and *Hist. of U. S.*
(Fin. Rev.), vi., 133, citing also *Journals of Congress*, iv., 481–2 ; Merriam,
Hist. of Ordinance, 14–5.   The resolution is in King's handwriting.

[2] The vote was :   *Aye*, N. H., Mass., R. I., Conn., N. Y., N. J., Penn.,
Md. ; *No*, Va., N. Car., S. Car.   Of Maryland, Henry and Hinsman voted
aye ; McHenry, *no.*   Of Virginia, Hardy and Lee (R. H.) voted *no ;* Grayson,
aye.   Delaware had no delegates present, and Georgia had but one.

[3] Printed in Bancroft, *Hist. of Formation of Const.*, i., 418, where is cited
Papers of Old Congress, xxxi., 329 ; endorsed in the handwriting of King :
" Report on Mr. King's motion for the exclusion of slavery in the new states."
Papers of Old Congress, xxxi., 331, is also cited.   *Cf.* Bancroft, *Hist. of U. S.*
(Fin. Rev.), vi., 133 ; Merriam, *Hist. of Ordinance*, 15–6.

March 15 that Mr. King intended to restore the provision in the draft of March 1, 1784, except the clause tolerating slavery for a time. The language is very similar, and the motion was to stand with the ordinance of April 23, 1784, as one of the principles of the " charter of compact." [1] The report has even a closer resemblance, for the clause extending the time of slavery until 1801 is added.

The source of the fugitive-slave clause or the occasion of its introduction is not known with certainty. A committee of northern men, from States where slavery was becoming more and more unpopular, would hardly have introduced such a provision without pressure from outside the committee. There must have been some occasion for inserting it. But without more evidence of the political side of the measures taken by the Old Congress at this time, it is unsafe to assign a cause. A precedent for such a provision, although one which there is little reason to believe the committee had in mind, is found in the Articles of Confederation between the plantations under the government of Massachusetts, New-Plymouth, Connecticut, and New Haven, of the year 1643.[2]

---

[1] Compare the original provision : " That after the year 1800 of the Christian Era *there shall be neither slavery nor involuntary servitude in any of the said States, otherwise than in punishment of crimes, whereof the party shall have been* duly convicted to have been *personally guilty.*" . . . . " *That* the preceding articles *shall be* formed into a charter of *compact,* . . . . and shall stand as *fundamental constitutions between the thirteen original states and* those newly described " : Above, Sec. IV., (a). Italicised words are those common to the motion of King and the draft of March 1, 1784. Jefferson speaks of King's motion as his own, in these words : " On the 16th of March, 1785, it was moved that the same proposition (which he had just mentioned as defeated) should be referred to a committee, and it was referred by the vote of eight states against three " : Washington, *Writings of Jefferson,* ix., 276.

[2] The clause relative to the same subject in this old document is as follows : "It is also agreed yt if any servante run away from his maister into another of these confederated jurisdictions, that in such case, upon ye certificate of one magistrate in ye jurisdiction out of which ye said servante fledd, or upon other due proofe, the said servante shall be delivered, either to his maister, or any other yt pursues & brings such certificate or proofe."—William Bradford's *History of Plymouth Plantations,* in *Mass. Hist. Coll.,* Fourth Series, iii., 421 ; all the " Articles," *Ibid.,* 416-23. After the above clause is a longer paragraph stipulating about the return of fugitive prisoners or criminals. *Cf.* on the subject in

The report of April 6 was assigned for consideration April 14, but as late as May, King was holding it until the land ordinance, then under way, should pass.[1]   It seems never to have been called up again as a separate measure.

general : Dunn, *Indiana*, 193; Bancroft, *Hist. of U. S.* (Fin. Rev.), vi., 133; and *Hist. of Formation of Const.*, i., 418 ; Stone, *Ordinance of 1787*, in *Penn. Mag. of Hist., and Biog.*, xiii., 315; *Ohio State Reports*, Critchfield, ix., 125 ; where the assertion is made that the clause was copied from the old compact; Merriam, *Hist. of Ordinance*, 15–16.

[1] Grayson to Madison, May 1, 1785 : " Mr. King, of Mass., has a resolution ready drawn, which he reserves till the ordinance is passed, for preventing slavery in the new state.   I expect seven states may be found liberal enough to adopt it " ; Bancroft, *Hist. of Formation of Const.*, i., 435.

VI.

PLANS FOR FEWER STATES.

(a)—*Monroe's Influence.*

Up to this point the man who had exerted the greatest influence in the matter of organizing the West was probably Jefferson. But in May, 1784, he left the halls of legislation for other work assigned him, and his personal influence ceased. James Monroe brought about the next change of ideas regarding the new territory. These two men were sent by their State to Congress in 1783.[1] Jefferson, however, had been connected with this body at its inception, and long since had become familiar with the questions with which it had to deal. He was thus prepared to take an active part in the schemes for the government of the West, when legislation to that end was attempted in 1784. On the other hand, Monroe was younger than Jefferson by fifteen years,[2] and had not that lively interest in matters of national concern which Jefferson showed. In 1785, however, Monroe became sufficiently interested in the new domain to visit the trans-Ohio lands, in order to investigate the subject for himself. In the summer of this year he indicated[3] to Jefferson his intention to attend the treaty-conference with the Indians, which was about to be held at the mouth of the Great Miami, and in August turned his

---

[1] Sparks, *Writings of Washington*, xii., 424 ; Linn, *Life of Jefferson*, 136.

[2] Randall, *Life of Jefferson*, i., 17 ; Gilman, *Monroe*, 4.

[3] July 15, 1785 : "I have it in contemplation, after a few weeks, to set out for the Ohio, to attend the treaty above mentioned" : Bancroft, *Hist. of Formation of Const.*, i., 445.

face westward.[1]   By December[2] he was again at his post in New York.

Whatever the views of Monroe may have been previous to this, no doubt now remained.   He had seen and he knew whereof he spoke.   He believed the previous measures of Congress regarding the division of the West into States had been impolitic: the interests of the Ohio valley would be very little connected with those of the Atlantic slope, and therefore the formation of many States would not tend to preserve the ascendancy of the East; the unproductiveness of the soil and the consequent slow development of the country showed also that a smaller number of new States should be formed.[3]   On this account Monroe took a firm stand for fewer States.   He believed that the congressional resolution of October 10, 1780, which limited districts to 150 miles square, had governed the division made in the ordinance of

---

[1] Monroe to Jefferson, New York, August 25, 1785 : *Ibid.*, 451.

[2] Letters dating in December : Bancroft, *Hist. of Formation of Const.*, i., 471, 475 ; *cf.*, *Writings of Madison*, i., 203.

[3] Monroe to Jefferson, New York, January 19, 1786 : " My several routes westward, with the knowledge of the country I have thereby obtained, have impressed me fully with the conviction of the impolicy of our measures respecting it.   I speak not in this instance of the ordinance for the survey and disposal of it, but of those which became necessary, and were founded upon the act of cession from the state of Virginia.   I am clearly of the opinion that to many of the most important objects of a federal government, their interests, if not opposed, will be but little connected with ours ; instead of weakening theirs and making it subservient to our purposes, we have given it all the possible strength we could ; weaken it we might also, and at the same time (I mean by reducing the number of states) render them substantial service.   A great part of the territory is miserably poor, especially that near Lakes Michigan and Erie ; and that upon the Mississippi and the Illinois consists of extensive plains which have not had, from appearances, and will not have a single bush on them for ages.   The districts, therefore, within which these fall, will, perhaps, never contain a sufficient number of inhabitants to entitle them to membership in the Confederacy, and in the meantime the people who may settle within them will be governed by the resolutions of Congress, in which they will not be represented."—Bancroft, *Hist. of Formation of Const.*, i., 480–1.   *Cf.*, Lee to Washington, October 11, 1785 : *Ibid.*, 460–1.   With this compare Jefferson's letter to Monroe, dated Paris, July 9, 1786, giving reasons why it would be well to make the states smaller and more numerous: Washington, *Works of Jefferson* (Edition of 1884), i., 586–8.

1784, and was still binding because incorporated into the deed of cession of Virginia.¹ After sounding members of Congress on the subject and finding them favorable,² he moved to refer the matter to a grand committee. In a report, March 24, 1786,³ it was recommended that the western lands be divided into not less than two nor more than five States, and that Virginia should revise her act of cession. By amendment the report was made to read : " That it be and hereby is recommended to the legislature of Virginia to take into consideration their act of cession and revise the same so far as to impower the United States in Congress assembled to make such a division of the territory of the United States lying northerly and westerly of the River Ohio into distinct republican states, not more than five nor less than three as the situation of that country and future circumstances may require."⁴ This was adopted as amended. It assigned various reasons for the change : " Whereas it appears . . . that the laying it out and forming it into states of the extent mentioned in the resolution of Congress of the tenth of October, 1780, and in one of the conditions contained in the cession of Virginia, will be productive of many and great inconveniences ; that by such a division of the country, some of the new states will be deprived of the advantages of navigation, some will be improperly intersected by lakes, rivers, and mountains, and some will contain too great a proportion of barren, unimprovable land, and of consequence will not for many years if ever have sufficient number of inhabitants to form a respectable government,

---

¹ Hening, *Statutes*, xi., 327, 572 ; Donaldson, *Public Domain*, 69 ; Chase, *Statutes of Ohio*, i., 62.

² Monroe to Madison, December 19, 1785 : '' I find the most enlightened members here . . . well inclined to a revision of the compact between the United States and Virginia respecting the division of the country beyond the Ohio '' : Bancroft, *Hist. of Formation of Const.*, i., 472.

³ Merriam, *Hist. of Ordinance*, 17 ; Bancroft, *Hist. of U. S.* (Fin. Rev.), vi., 278, citing *Papers of Old Congress*, xxx., 75 ; *Hist. of Formation of Const.*, ii., 99, 100 ; Donaldson, *Public Domain*, 150 ; Force, *History of Ordinance*, in *St. Clair Papers*, ii., 607, and *Life of Cutler*, ii., 412.

⁴ Merriam, *Hist. of Ordinance*, 17-8, citing *Journals of Congress*, iv., 663.

and entitle them to a seat and voice in the federal council:
And whereas in fixing the limits and dimensions of the new
states, due attention ought to be paid to natural boundaries
and a variety of circumstances which will be pointed out by
a more perfect knowledge of the country, so as to provide
for the future growth and prosperity of each state, as well
as for the accommodation and security of the first adven-
turers." [1]

Monroe did not embody his political reasons, but his hand
is easily traced.   The act of 1780 had also been cited by
Massachusetts in her deed of cession,[2] and as if at this further thought the same committee brought forth a second
report.[3] Virginia and Massachusetts were recommended to
revise their acts of cession, and thereafter Congress was to
have no restriction upon its power to divide the northwestern territory into states, except one providing that "the
said territory shall be divided into not less than two and not
more than five states."   From this it would appear that the
original idea of the committee regarding the number of new
states was preferred.

The Ordinance of 1784 was still in force.   The motion of
Rufus King in 1785 was supplementary to it.   But this
movement of Monroe meant more and portended a complete
revision of the law for the West.   Soon a committee was
appointed[4] to consider and report the form of a temporary

---

[1] Merriam, *Hist. of Ordinance*, 17.

[2] In the acts and deed of Massachusetts the resolve of Congress was only
cited as the one according to which the cession was made and the lands were
expected to be disposed of. *Cf.* Hening, *Statutes*, xi., 327,572 ; *Laws of
the Commonwealth of Mass.* (1807), i., 215, 241. Virginia embodied the language of the resolve of 1780, defining how large the new States should be.

[3] Bancroft, *Hist. of U. S.* (Fin. Rev.), vi., 278, cites the report itself in *Papers of Old Congress*, xxx., 79 ff., as not dated at all. The substance of the
report Monroe states in writing to Jefferson, May 11, 1786 : " A proposition,
or rather a report, is before Congress, recommending it to Virginia and Massachusetts to revise their acts as to that condition, so as to leave it to the United
States to make what division of the same, future circumstances may make
necessary, subject to this proviso : 'that the said territory be divided into not
less than two and not more than five states.' "—Bancroft, *Hist. of Formation
of Const.*, i., 502–3.

[4] This was by a motion of Nathan Dane of Massachusetts. The motion is

government.   At the head of this committee was Monroe, with William S. Johnson, Rufus King, John Kean, and Charles Pinckney.' The last two were from South Carolina, and Johnson from Connecticut.   The importance of their report on May 10, 1786,' as the point of departure in a new scheme of government for the West, seems to have been overlooked.   It has already been noted that as early as the discussions on the plan of March 1, 1784, Jacob Read of South Carolina proposed to have Congress appoint magistrates to govern the western country, or districts of it, in its first stage.'   The report of a committee now gave specific form to that idea.   Congress was to appoint governor, council, judges, secretary to the council,' and other officers. The council was composed of five members, and the court of five judges.   Common law and chancery jurisdiction were given to the court, and an existing code of laws was to be adopted.   And not only did this report supply the part which the plan of two years before lacked, but it went further.   The law of 1784 provided that a new State would have to begin by using the constitution and laws of one of the old States, with a legislature to alter the laws, composed of members representing counties; a permanent government might be organized when a district reached 20,000 popu-

---

thought by Dr. Bancroft to have been made in April, for which he cites *Papers of Old Congress*, xxx., 85 : *Hist. of U. S.* (Fin. Rev.), vi., 278, and *Hist. of Formation of Const.*, ii., 100, note 3 ; Winsor, *Narr. and Crit. Hist. of Amer.*, vii., 537.

¹ Bancroft, *Hist. of U. S.* (Fin. Rev.), vi., 278-79, and *Hist. of Formation of Const.*, ii., 100 ; Donaldson, *Public Domain*, 150 ; Force, *Hist. of Ordinance*, in *St. Clair Papers*, ii., 607, and *Life of Cutler*, ii., 412.

² Bancroft, *Hist. of U. S.* (Fin. Rev.), vi., 279, and *Hist. of Formation of Const.*, ii., 100-1 ; Winsor, *Narr. and Crit. Hist. of Amer.*, vii., 537, citing *Journals of Congress*, v., 79 ; Force, *Hist. of Ordinance*, in *St. Clair Papers*, ii., 607, and *Life of Cutler*, ii., 412 ; Donaldson, *Public Domain*, 150.   But by far the most valuable information on this comes from a letter of Monroe to Jefferson, dated New York, May 11, 1786, only the next day after the report of the plan : Bancroft, *Hist. of Formation of Const.*, i., 502-3.

³ Above, Sec. IV. (b).

⁴ Stone, *Ordinance of 1787*, in *Penn. Mag. of Hist. and Biog.*, xiii., 316, has "Secretary for the territory or states."

lation, and it might be admitted when its population reached that of the least numerous of the original States.   There
were now to be two distinct stages of government, and the
first should begin with adopted laws.   But the most striking
change is in the appointment of officers.   By the existing
law, the temporary organization of a district should be
made by its inhabitants convened for that purpose.   It was
here proposed that Congress appoint the chief officers.   In
its second stage which was allowed when a certain population was reached, a legislature elected by the State was to
be added to governor and council, forming a general assembly.   The delegate with half privilege was added, just as it
had been provided in the draft of March 1, 1784.[1]   The requirement for admission to the Confederation was the same
as in the law of 1784.   The progress lately made in the
manner of dividing the West was saved in the report;[2] but
slavery found no mention.[3]

(b)—*Grayson's Influence.*

Here the matter rested for a time.   In the next move that
affected the substance of Monroe's report the influence of
another member from Virginia produced excellent results.
The solitary "aye" of William Grayson in the vote of Virginia on Rufus King's slavery motion,[4] five days after enter-
ing Congress, showed not only his independence but some-

[1] Above, Sec. IV., (a).

[2] Bancroft, *Hist. of U. S.* (Fin. Rev.), vi., 279, and *Hist. of Formation of Const.*, ii., 100; Winsor, *Narr. and Crit. Hist. of Amer.*, vii., 537, citing *Journals of Congress*, v., 79.

[3] Here was an excellent opportunity for Monroe and others on the committee to show their principles regarding slavery.   Although Monroe was chairman of the committee, the failure to mention slavery in the report cannot be ascribed to him alone.   It is perhaps singular that before, when slavery came up for decision, he was first sick and again absent ; but with these three cases only, the inference of Bancroft, that Monroe was avoiding difficulties, is hardly warranted.   King was on the committee also, from whom something might have been expected.   *Cf.* Bancroft, *Hist. of U. S.* (Fin. Rev.), vi., 279, and *Hist. of Formation of Const.*, ii., 101.

[4] Above, Sec. V. ; Bancroft, *Hist. of U. S.* (Fin. Rev.), vi., 133, and *Hist. of Formation of Const.*, i., 179.

what of his general character; and now a second time he showed his good judgment and freedom from local spirit. Monroe had again pressed the question of diminishing the number of new States to be formed, and the grand committee having his motion under consideration reported July 7, 1786,[1] that the assent of Virginia should be obtained, to divide the territory northwest of the Ohio into not less than two nor more than five States. The same had been twice advised in the spring. The report brought the matter before Congress for discussion, and Grayson moved[2] to divide the territory in the following manner: An east and west line touching the most southern point of Lake Michigan should separate the territory into two parts. There should be three States between this line and the Ohio, formed by meridians at the mouth of the Wabash and Great Miami rivers. Lake Michigan divided the country north of the line into two parts, and these were to be States.[3] The idea was to have not less than five. The southern members favored this, the northern opposed, and the motion was lost. But upon the motion to divide ultimately into at least three States, there was general agreement.[4] Why the North opposed and the South favored a larger number of States, is not plain on the surface. Indeed, Monroe had already favored a diminution of the number of States partly for political reasons.[5] There was a curious variety of opinions among the members, growing out of local jealousy and the Mississippi question. In the South there was much sympathy with the West in their demand for the free navigation of the Mississippi, and a goodly array of new States, it was thought, would aid their endeavors. An idea which had influenced the South before, may also have had weight now,—that in the development

---

[1] Bancroft, *Hist. of U. S.* (Fin. Rev.), vi., 280, and *Hist. of Formation of Const.*, ii., 102.

[2] Bancroft, *Hist. of U. S.* (Fin. Rev.), vi., 280, and *Hist. of Formation of Const.*, ii., 102.

[3] See Map III.

[4] Bancroft, *Hist. of U. S.* (Fin. Rev.), vi., 280, and *Hist. of Formation of Const.*, ii., 103, citing *Journals of Congress*, iv., 662-3.

[5] Above, Sec. VI.

of the West, the southern vote in Congress would be increased, rather than the northern.[1] Conservative ideas prevailed among the northern men, especially those from New England, and they failed to give cordial support to measures encouraging development of the West. A number of circumstances favored the project of Mr. Jay to close the Mississippi : the North opposed the South for local reasons; northern States had lands of their own to settle ; they were afraid that the settlements in the West would draw away their population so as to diminish their power in Congress; and the failure of North Carolina and Georgia to cede provoked general hostility.[2]

If these sentiments of northern and southern men account for their positions on the question of dividing the West into States, they probably have quite as much to do with the fact that the whole scheme of Monroe failed to be acted upon at this time. Here Monroe's personal influence ends. He wrote to Jefferson about the middle of July : " This (the plan of government) hath not been decided on, and hath only been postponed in consequence of the inordinate schemes of some men above alluded to, as to the whole policy of the affairs of that country. . . . In October I shall leave this for Virginia, and shall settle in Fredricksburg for the purpose of commencing the practice of law."[3]

---

[1] Elliot's *Debates*, iii., 311, 312, 334-50 : a general discussion of the Mississippi question from these points of view, by Madison, Monroe, and Grayson. *Cf.* Stone, *Ordinance of 1787*, in *Penn. Mag. of Hist. and Biog.*, xiii., 329-32 ; Gilman, *Monroe*, 25-26 ; McMaster, *Hist. of People of U. S.*, i., 378.

[2] Bancroft, *Hist. of U. S.* (Fin. Rev.) vi., 280, and *Hist. of Formation of Const.*, ii., 103 ; Dunn, *Indiana*, 194-5 ; see Bancroft, *Hist. of Formation of Const.*, i. and ii., printed letters and papers, *passim ; e. g.*, Otto to Vergennes, September 10, 1786, *Ibid.*, ii., 389-93. Monroe wrote to Madison, December 19, 1785, that he found the " most enlightened members " of Congress "doubtful of the propriety of admitting a single new one into the Confederacy " : *Ibid.*, i., 471-2. Washington wrote, April 25, 1785, in answer to a letter of Grayson : "and (under the rose) a penetrating eye and close observation will discover, through various disguises, a disinclination to add new states to the confederation westward of us " : *Ibid.*, i., 431-2. *Cf.* Bancroft, *Hist. of Formation of Const. ;* ii., 431.

[3] July 16, 1786 : Bancroft, *Hist. of Formation of Const.*, ii., 373. *Cf. ibid.*, 103, and *Hist. of U. S.* (Fin. Rev.), vi., 281.

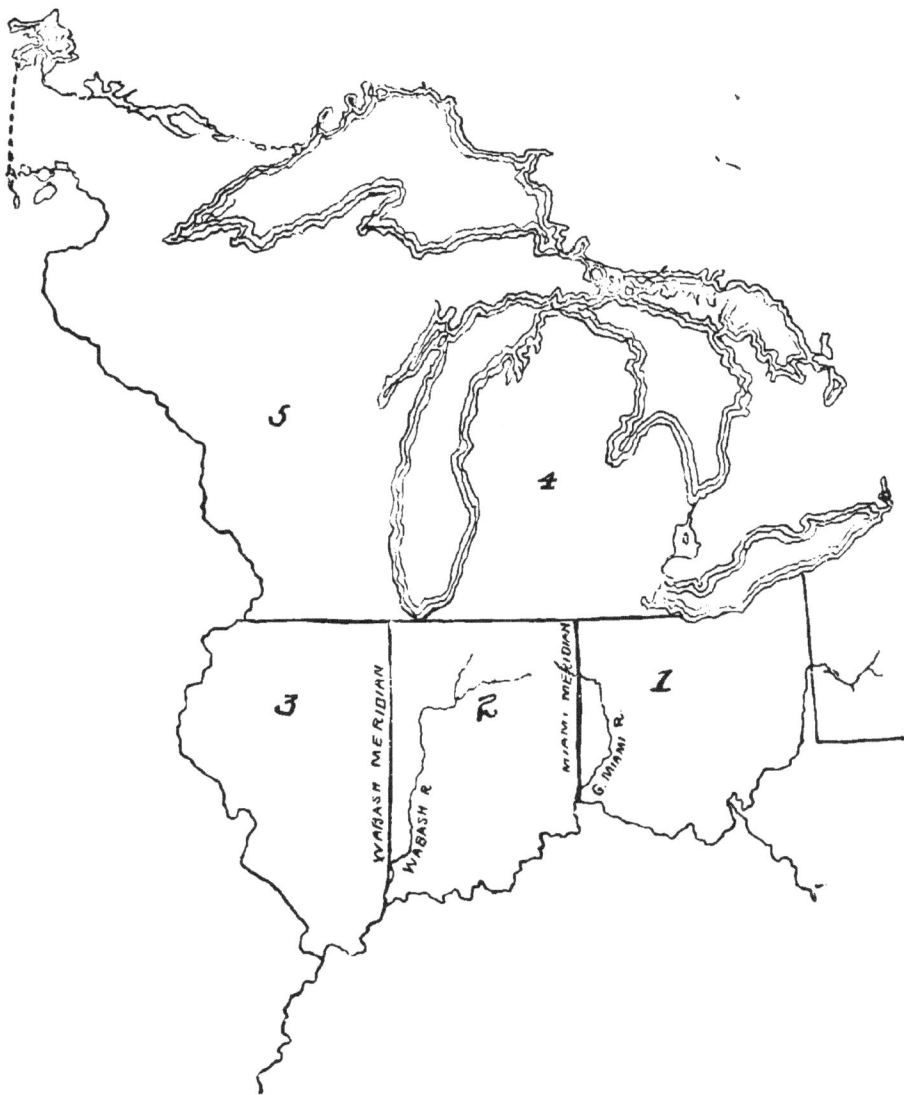

III.

DIVISION ACCORDING TO GRAYSON'S MOTION,
JULY 7, 1786.

A motion of Grayson during the spring on a subject touching western affairs, and ultimately provided for in the territorial constitution, must here be noticed. It was connected with this very subject of the Mississippi, which then entered so largely into congressional politics. Tax was forbidden for navigating the tributaries of the Mississippi and St. Lawrence. The Mississippi question was not here settled; but so far as this proposition of Grayson was concerned, the Northeast could not object: Rufus King seconded the motion.[1] This move, traceable perhaps to the discussion of the boundaries of new States, proclaimed a definite policy for the general government with regard to freedom of navigation, which it was not slow to adopt.

From the work of William Grayson in 1786, therefore, came two important suggestions for the constitution of the territory: the clause proclaiming free navigation, and the idea of dividing the Northwest into five States having certain boundaries.

---

[1] Bancroft, *Hist. of U. S.* (Fin. Rev.), vi., 279, and *Hist. of Formation of Const.*, ii., 101.

VII.

THE NORTHERN COMMITTEE.

(a)—*The First Report.*

The absence of Monroe, King, and Kean for various reasons and at different times during the summer of 1786 rendered it necessary to put new men on the committee.[1] Johnson succeeded to the chairmanship, and his new associates were Melancthon Smith, John Henry, and Nathan Dane. These three represented respectively New York, Maryland, and Massachusetts. Their report was presented September 19, 1786,[2] and the part relating to the administration of the oath was discussed September 29;[3] but it was not acted upon at the time. The plan reported by Monroe was the basis, but these differences are noted : the court was to consist of three members; the requirement for a second stage of territorial government was " 5,000 free male adults residing within a district " ; the payment of part of the Federal debt by the new State was repeated from the

---

[1] Melancthon Smith appears as one of the committee in August, probably *vice* Kean, who was gone during the summer : Bancroft, *Hist. of U. S.* (Fin. Rev.), vi., 281, citing *Journals of Cong.*, iv., 688-9. *Cf.* Stone, *Ordinance of 1787*, in *Penn. Mag. of Hist. and Biog.*, xiii., 316.

[2] Bancroft, *Hist. of U. S.* (Fin. Rev.), vi., 281, and *Hist. of Formation of Const.*, ii., 104 ; Force, *Hist. of Ordinance*, in *St. Clair Papers*, ii., 607, and *Life of Cutler*, ii., 412 ; Donaldson, *Public Domain*, 150 ; Stone, *Ordinance of 1787*, in *Penn. Mag. of Hist. and Biog.*, xiii., 316, where September 21 is given ; Sato, *Land Question*, 91, citing *Journals of Cong.*, iv., 701-2 ; *Ohio Arch. and Hist. Quar.*, ii., 38.

[3] Bancroft, in his Final Revision, vi., 281, has the same difference from other authorities as in his earlier work, *Hist. of Formation of Const.*, ii., 104, putting this September 30, 1786. *Cf.* Sato, *Land Question*, 91, citing *Journals of Cong.*, iv., 701-2.

enactment of 1784; and the requirement for admission to the Union was raised to one thirteenth of the whole population of the original States and consent of Congress. The last item is probably the most important in showing the political bias of the committee.[1] A majority were northern men, and they voiced the ideas of their section. The drafting was done largely by Dane, assisted by Pinckney on the part relating to temporary government.[2] The presence of Dane accounts for an innovation here. There now appeared in the report provisions touching the descent and conveyance of estates. It was provided that "the real estates of the resident proprietors, dying intestate previous to the organization of the general assembly, shall descend to the heir of such proprietors, male and female, in equal parts; . . . provided however that such proprietors shall be at liberty to dispose of such lands by alienation, by bargain and sale, testamentary devise, or otherwise as he shall think proper."[3] Mr. Dane's later course makes it extremely probable that he caused the insertion of this. An important provision securing the benefits of the writ of *habeas corpus* and trial by jury was also added. It is found in most of the bills of rights or constitutions of the States,[4] and was thought to be important and necessary.

This report of the autumn of 1786 appears to be the point of departure in adding to the plan of western government a bill of rights and a complete law regarding estates.

(b)—*The Second Report.*

A period of seven months intervened before the subject again received the attention of Congress, and that body meanwhile underwent some changes in its membership.

---

[1] Monroe, writing to Jefferson in July, shows that the endeavor at that time on the part of some was to raise the requirement for admission : Bancroft, *Hist. of Formation of Const.*, ii., 371–2.

[2] Dane, in the ninth volume of his *Abridgment* (1830), Appendix, 74–5 : King, *Ohio*, 405–9.

[3] Merriam, *Hist. of Ordinance*, 20.

[4] *Cf.* Poore, *Charters*, 382–3, 817, 958–9, 1410, 1909, etc.

The committee of September, however, were all on hand at the next session and presented a report on April 26, 1787.[1] At its second reading on May 9, the committee's work on requirement for admission was undone,[2] and the subject of territorial representation was debated.[3] The next day was set for its third reading. This plan,[4] when ready for its final consideration, provided for the northwestern country a complete political organization. During the first stage there should be a governor, a secretary to keep the records of the executive and legislative departments, and furnish the secretary of Congress periodically with copies of acts and proceedings, and a court of three judges with common-law jurisdiction. The term of the governor was to be three years, that of the secretary four, while the judges were to hold office during good behavior. The governor and judges were also to constitute a quasi-legislative body, to adopt criminal and civil laws from the original States, and publish them in the district. It was their duty to report to Congress whatever laws they adopted ; and in case that body did not disapprove, the adopted laws should be in force as long as that stage of the temporary government lasted. The functions of Chief Executive were in other respects those usually belonging to that office. In the second stage, which

---

[1] Winsor, *Narr. and Crit. Hist. of Amer.*, vii., 537 ; Bancroft, *Hist. of U. S.* (Fin. Rev.), vi., 281–2, and *Hist. of Formation of Const.*, ii., 104 ; Force, *Hist. of Ordinance*, in *St. Clair Papers*, ii., 607, and *Life of Cutler*, ii., 413 ; Stone, *Ordinance of 1787*, in *Penn. Mag. of Hist. and Biog.*, xiii., 317 ; but Dunn, *Indiana*, 195, has April 23 ; Sato, *Land Question*, 91 ; Merriam, *Hist. of Ordinance*, 19.

[2] Bancroft, *Hist. of U. S.* (Fin. Rev.), 282, and *Hist. of Formation of Const.*, ii., 105, arguing from erasures on the printed bill ; Sato, *Land Question*, 91. But the copy in Force's *Hist. of the Ordinance* has the provision in it.

[3] Sato, *Land Question*, 91, citing *Journals of Cong.*, iv., 746.

[4] The form of the Ordinance as it was ordered to a third reading was published by Peter Force in the *National Intelligencer* of August 26, 1847, and is found also in *Western Law Journal*, v., 529: Winsor, *Narr. and Crit. Hist. of Amer.*, vii., 537, note 2 ; Sato, *Land Question*, 92 ; Adams, *Maryland's Influence*, 46, and *Nation*, xxxiv., 384. Also printed in Force's *Hist. of Ordinance* in *St. Clair Papers*, ii., App. i., and *Life of Cutler*, ii., App. D, 413–6 : Merriam, *Hist. of Ordinance*, 21–3 ; Donaldson, *Public Domain*, 150–2.

might take place as soon as there were "five thousand free male inhabitants of full age" within the district, a house of representatives was added. Its members were to be elected by the people, one for every 500 free male inhabitants, and together with the governor and a legislative council of five to be appointed by Congress, should constitute the general assembly. Representatives and their electors were to have a property qualification ; but it was not prescribed for governor and secretary. Members of the house of representatives held office two years ; those of the council continued during the pleasure of Congress. The governor had absolute veto on all bills passed by the two legislative bodies, and power to convene, prorogue, and dissolve the assembly when he found it expedient. Of general principles the report contained the rights of *habeas corpus* and of trial by jury, and required that the lands of non-residents should not be taxed higher than those of residents. Furthermore, the inhabitants would have to pay a share of the Federal debts. The territory to be organized by this proposed law is not specified, but the amended title shows that the entire northwestern country was to form one district. It was first called " An ordinance for the government of the western territory " ; but was amended to read, " An ordinance for the government of the territory of the United States, northwest of the River Ohio, until the same shall be divided into different States." Afterwards the second clause was struck out.[1]

---

[1] Merriam, *Hist. of Ordinance*, 21.

VIII.

THE OHIO COMPANY.

The third reading of this ordinance was fixed for the next day, May 10.[1] On that day the order of business was called by Massachusetts; but the question of adjournment for a short vacation and change of place of meeting to Philadelphia took precedence, and the regular order was postponed.[2] On May 9 the Ohio Company applied for a purchase of lands in the northwestern territory. The first movements in the organization of this company were made early in 1786,[3] and articles were drawn in March. A year later three directors were chosen, Gen. Samuel A. Parsons, Gen. Rufus Putnam, and the Rev. Manasseh Cutler.[4] The first was entrusted with the business of purchasing lands for the whole company, and it was he who now appeared with a memorial for that purpose. It was immediately referred to a committee of five: Edward Carrington, Rufus King, Nathan Dane, James Madison, and Egbert Benson.[5] Some writers have thought that there existed a necessary connection between the memorial of the Ohio Company, presented May 9, and the failure of the ordinance to be acted on May 10. But there appears no necessity for so interpreting the events.[6]

---

[1] *Journals of Congress*, iv., 747 ; Bancroft, *Hist. of U. S.* (Fin. Rev.), vi. 282, and *Hist. of Formation of Const.*, ii., 105.

[2] Merriam, *Hist. of Ordinance*, 20.

[3] *Life of Cutler*, i., 179 ; *N. A. Review*, liii., 331 (October, 1841) ; *Ohio Arch. and Hist. Quar.*, ii., 80.

[4] *Life of Cutler*, i., 191-2.

[5] Bancroft, *Hist. of U. S.* (Fin. Rev.), vi., 285, and *Hist. of Formation of Const.*, ii., 110.

[6] *Cf.* Bancroft, *Hist. of U. S.* (Fin. Rev.), vi., 282-5, and *Hist. of Formation of Const.*, ii., 105-10 ; Dunn, *Indiana*, 201-2.

On May 11 the ordinance failed to be called up, and
there was no chance for a consideration of it from May 12
to July 4, since Congress did not meet in that interval.
On the anniversary of Independence day a quorum had
gathered at the hall in New York, and the day seems to
have been largely occupied with preliminary organization.
At least in the absence of Gen. Arthur St. Clair, the
regular president, William Grayson was chosen to fill his
place for the time.[1]   A day of no quorum intervened, and
on July 6 Congress began business again.   The directors
of the Ohio Company were on the lookout for this,[2] and
before legislation had been fairly commenced, one of the
directors was present to press vigorously the suit of the
Ohio Company for the purchase of land.   It was Manasseh
Cutler, whose name has lately gained an inseparable connection with the ordinance enacted by Congress during the
next week.   He arrived on the evening of Thursday, July
5,[3] and on the following morning opened his business with
Congress.   This New England divine, without doubt, was
amply qualified to effect his purpose.   He was a man of
large experience, combining common sense with genial
manners, and well understanding how to deal with men.   In
his possession were letters of introduction to many members of Congress, which he forthwith delivered, and ere long
he was on the inside of the congressional circle.   The
memorial of Cutler was immediately referred to a committee
whose membership is supposed to have been the same
as in the case of Putnam's petition.   This is affirmed 'on the

---

[1] Bancroft, *Hist. of U. S.* (Fin. Rev.), vi., 285, and *Hist. of Formation of
Const.*, ii., 110.

[2] Cutler to Sargent, Boston, May 30, 1789 : *Life of Cutler*, i., 196.

[3] Cutler's Diary, July 5 : *Life of Cutler*, i., 228.   In both editions of his
works, Bancroft has Friday, July 5 :   *Hist. of U. S.* (Fin. Rev.), vi., 286, and
Hist. of Formation of Const., ii., 110.

[4] Bancroft, *Hist. of U. S.* (Fin. Rev.), vi., 286, and *Hist. of Formation of
Const.*, ii., 111.   He states that the report is to be found in vol. v. of the
Reports of Committees and in *Old Papers of Congress*, xix., 27 ; and that the
report is in the handwriting of Edward Carrington and indorsed :   "Report of
Committee on Memorial of S. H. Parsons," and that it is further indorsed in the

ground that the report is indorsed with the names of the same committee.   But the question arises how Mr. King and Mr. Madison could help to make the report while they were in Philadelphia.   On the day the subject was referred and also on July 10, the day of the reading of the report, both took part in the debates at the Convention in Philadelphia.'   It is not probable that such an important matter as the large purchase contemplated by the Ohio Company would be referred to a committee, nearly half of whom are known to have been permanently absent.

hand of Mr. Thompson, " Report of Mr. Carrington, Mr. King, Mr. Dane, Mr. Madison, Mr. Benson.   Read July 10, 1787.   Order of the day for the eleventh." Mr. Bancroft thinks that Cutler, in stating that a committee was appointed July 6, was mistaken.   *Cf.* Cutler's *Diary*, July 6 : *Life of Cutler*, i., 230.

¹ Elliot's *Debates*, v., 280, 282, 290, 292.

IX.

THE FINAL COMMITTEE.

BIBLIOGRAPHICAL NOTE FOR THE SUBJECT OF THE ORDINANCE OF 1787.
—J. M. Merriam, *Legislative Hist. of the Ordinance of 1787*, 23–42 ; F.
D. Stone, *The Ordinance of 1787*, in *Penn. Mag. of Hist. and Biog.*, xiii.,
309–40 ; W. F. Poole, *Dr. Cutler and the Ordinance of 1787*, in *No. Am. Rev.*,
vol. 122, pp. 229–65 ; J. P. Dunn, Jr., *Indiana* (Commonwealth Series), 195–
215 ; Shosuke Sato, *Hist. of the Land Question in the U. S.* (J. H. U. Studies,
Fourth Series, vii.–ix.), 93–117 ; George Bancroft, *Hist. of U. S.* (Fin. Rev.),
vi., 286–90, and *Hist. of Formation of Const.*, ii., 110–16 ; Peter Force, *Ordinance of 1787 and its History*, in *St. Clair Papers*, ii., 610–18, and *Life of
Cutler*, ii., 417–27 ; Thomas Donaldson, *Public Domain*, 152–6 ; W. H. Smith,
St. Clair Papers, i., 118–36 ; Cutler's Diary, *Life of Cutler*, i., 228–42, 298 ;
Rufus King, *Ohio* (Commonwealth Series), 180–8 ; B. A. Hinsdale, *Old North-
west*, 268–79 ; W. W. Williams, *Arthur St. Clair and the Ordinance of 1787*,
in *Mag. West. Hist.*, i., 53–61 ; I. W. Andrews, *The Northwest Territory*, in
Mag. Amer. Hist., xv., 141–5 ; Richard Hildreth, *Hist. of U. S.*, iii., 527–9 ;
J. T. Curtis, *Hist. of Const.*, i., 301–8, 452, note 2 ; ii., 344–5 ; J. B.
McMaster, *Hist. of the People of U. S.*, i., 507–8 ; ii., 478 ; Thomas Cooley,
Michigan (Commonwealth Series), 127–32, 138 ; J. B. Dillon, *Hist. of Indiana*,
202–3, 539–40, 597–601 ; I. W. Andrews, *Beginnings of Our Colonial System*,
in *Ohio Arch. and Hist. Quar.*, i., 10–37 ; Nathan Dane :—(1) Letter to Rufus
King, July 16, 1787 : Bancroft, *Hist. of Formation of Const.*, ii., 430–31, *Life
of Cutler*, i., 371–3, Spencer, *Hist. of U. S.*, ii., 208–9 ; (2) Letter to Daniel
Webster, March 26, 1830, in *Mass. Hist. Soc. Proc.*, 1867–69, 475–80 ; (3)
Letter to J. H. Farnham, May 21, 1831, printed in *New York Tribune*, June
18, 1875 : quoted in part by Merriam, *Legislative Hist. of Ordinance of 1787*,
37 ; (4) "*Abridgment*," vii., 389, ix., App., 74–76 : King, *Ohio*, 405–9 ;
Bryant and Gay, *Pop. Hist. of U. S.*, iv., 95, 110 ; *Penn. Archives*, xi., 162–8 ;
Henry Wilson, *Rise and Fall of Slave Power*, i., 31–8 ; J. W. Monette, *Hist.
of Disc. and Settlement of Valley of Mississippi*, ii., 237–40 ; *Bulletin of U. S.
Geol. Survey*, No. 13, p. 28 ; Davidson and Stuvé, *Hist. of Illinois*, 207, 210–
12 ; Staples, *Rhode Island in the Cont. Cong.*, 571–2 ; Ford, *Hist. of Illinois*,
20 ; J. W. Taylor, *Hist. of State of Ohio, First Period, 1650–1787*, 497–515,
551–7 ; *Land Laws of U. S.* (Ed. 1828), 356 : Winsor, *Narr. and Crit. Hist.
of Amer.*, vii., 538, and Taylor, *Hist. of State of Ohio*, 551 ; J. R. Albach,
Annals of the West, 460–72 ; J. H. Perkins, *Annals of the West*, 293–8 ; *Life

of Cutler, i., 342–71 ; W. W. Williams, *Hist. of Negro Race in Amer.*, i.,
416–7 ; J. C. Ridpath, *Pop. Hist. of U. S. of Amer.* (Ed. 1889), 359 ; John
Fiske, *Crit. Period of Amer. Hist.*, 199, 202–7 ; *Civil Government of U. S.*,
90, 253, 255 ; W. F. Poole, *Gen. Arthur St. Clair*, in (Chicago) *Dial*, ii., 252–
3 ; and *Gen. Arthur St. Clair and the Ordinance of 1787*, in *Ibid.*, iii., 14–15 ;
W. H. Smith, *Gen. Arthur St. Clair and the Ordinance of 1787*, in *Ibid.*, ii.,
294–6 ; G. W. Knight, *Hist. of Land Grants for Education in N. W.
Territory*, in *Papers of Amer. Hist. Assoc.*, Vol. i., No. 3, pp. 15, 16 ; L. H.
Porter, *Outlines of Const. Hist. of U. S.*, 62–9 ; N. W. Edwards, *Hist. of
Illinois, 1778–1833, and Life and Times of Ninian Edwards*, 8–11 ; D. W.
Howe, *The Laws and Courts of the Northwest and Indiana Territories*, in
Ind. Hist. Soc. Pamphlets, No. 1, pp. 3–5 : C. M. Walker, *Hist of Athens Co.,
Ohio*, 53–69, 88, 90–2 ; I. W. Andrews, *Manual of Const. of U. S.*, 296–7 ;
App., xiii.–xix. ; Cooper, *Amer. Politics*, Bk. iv., 10–13 ; H. B. Adams, *Mary-
land's Influence upon Land Cessions to U. S.*, (J. H. U. Studies, Third Series),
i., 45–54, and *Nation*, May 4, 1882 ; Alex. Johnson, *Ordinance of 1787*, in
Lalor's Cyc. of Pol. Sci., iii., 30–2 ; cf. *Ibid.*, 735, 919–20 ; Von Holst, *Const.
Hist. of U. S.*, 1750–1832, 37, 288 ; S. O. Griswold, in *West. Reserve Hist.
Soc. Tracts*, ii., 288–9 ; Timothy Pitkin, *Pol. and Civ. Hist. of U. S. of Amer.*,
ii., 211 ; William Goodell, *Slavery and Anti-Slavery*, 83 ; Landon, *Const. Hist.
and Gov't. of U. S.*, 99, 185–6 ; Samuel Eliot, *Manual of U. S. Hist.*, 275 ;
Arnold, *Hist. of State of R. I.*, ii., 539 ; Lucien Carr, *Missouri* (Common-
wealth Series), 57 ; Atwater, *Hist. of State of Ohio*, 126–7 ; J. A. Spencer.
Hist. of U. S., ii., 202–4, 206–9 ; Campbell, *Pol. Hist. of Mich.*, 206–10 ;
Farmer, *Hist. of Detroit and Mich.*, 85–6 ; *Library of Univ. Knowledge*, xi.,
39 ; *Ohio Arch. and Hist. Quar.*, ii., No. 1, pp. 17, 25, 36, 38–49, 54, 81–3,
92, 153–6, 194–6, 224 ; Lanman, *Hist. of Mich.*, 166–7 ; Carpenter and Arthur,
Hist. of Illinois, 109 ; *Mich. Pioneer and Hist. Coll.*, vii., 18 ; xi., 140–44 ;
Schuckers, *Life and Pub. Services of S. P. Chase*, 58–60 ; Moses, *Illinois, His-
torical and Statistical*, i., 185–91 ; Alexander Johnston, *United States*, 83–86.

Bibliographies are given in Howard, *Local Const. Hist. of U. S.*, i., 142,
note 3, and 410, note 2 ; Winsor, *Narr. and Crit. Hist. of Amer.*, vii., 537–8.

(a)—*Membership.*

The energy of the Ohio Company's agent bid fair to
leave no opportunity to consider other matters until the
purchase was effected ; but Congress determined at last to
finish the plan that had so long been preparing and had
been changed so many times. July 9, 1787,[1] the subject
was finally referred to a new committee. Johnson, Pinckney, and Henry were away, leaving only two members of

[1] Bancroft, *Hist. of U. S.* (Fin. Rev.), vi., 286, and *Hist. of Formation of
Const.*, ii., 111, 112. The ground for supposing this is an endorsement on one
of the papers in the State department.

the last committee present. These two, Nathan Dane and
Melancthon Smith, were reappointed together with Edward
Carrington, Richard H. Lee, and John Kean, who had
served on a similar committee just a year before. The
choice of these men seems not in the least peculiar. Mr.
Kean would be expected to be familiar with the subject and
thus render substantial aid. R. H. Lee had taken his place
in Congress the very day on which the committee was
appointed. He had presided over that body in 1784 and
1785,[1] and was therefore a prominent member. Dane
regarded his advent with satisfaction, and it is not surprising that Congress gave him committee work at the first
opportunity. Carrington was one of the influential and
pushing members of this Congress, chairman of the committee on purchase of land appointed in May,[2] and familiar
with western affairs. The further question has arisen, why
Carrington was made chairman. There appears nothing
positive. Possibly because he was already chairman of the
committee on land purchase, or because the southern
members, having a majority, wished to keep the lead in
important matters. It is thought singular that Dane should
not have filled this place, since he had been prominent for
some time in the discussions of this subject. It might as
well be asked why this office was not conferred on Mr.
Smith, who had been serving on the committee longer than
Mr. Dane.[3] In the important committees the chairman
was quite generally an influential member, as were those
who had been at the head of the several committees on
western government, viz.: Thomas Jefferson, James
Monroe, and William Johnson. Nathan Dane was admira-
bly fitted for his share of the work. Hardly another would
have done the work as he did it. But on account of his
provincialism he was not one such as might be expected to
be made chairman.

[1] Sparks, *Writings of Washington*, xii., 420.
[2] Above, Sec. VIII.
[3] Mr. Smith was first connected with a committee at least as early as August,
1786 ; Dane probably began in September. *Cf.* above, Sec. VII.

Thus constituted, the last committee of the Old Congress on the subject of western territorial government made a final trial at the task.

(b)—*Work of the Committee.*

Apparently something had been attempted before the appointment of the new committee.[1] The proposal to settle the Western country caused a desire to get a better plan of government than had yet been devised for it, and the language of Mr. Dane at least suggests a general demand on the part of the land purchasers for such a thing.[2] However that may be, new ideas came to the front and a new set of men was placed in charge. Their report was made July 11. From the ninth to the eleventh of that month, therefore, the work was accomplished. There is record of the amendments made when the report was before Congress, so that the work done by the committee is known. What share did each of the committee have in framing the report? To whom shall be ascribed the suggestion of the new features? An answer must be based either upon the statements of those who had opportunity to know, or upon the evidence drawn from the report itself, or upon both.

, There seems no reason to doubt that the part of drawing up the report was taken by Nathan Dane.[3] He asserted it

---

[1] Dane to King, New York, July 16, 1787 : "We tried one day to patch up M.'s system of western government ; started new ideas and committed the whole to Carrington, Dane. R. H. Lee, Smith, and Kean " : Bancroft, *Hist. of Formation of Const.*, ii., 431 ; *Life of Cutler*, i., 371 ; Dunn, *Indiana*, 206. *Life of Cutler* has " M. S. P. systems of W. government."

[2] " We found ourselves rather pressed ; the Ohio Company appeared to purchase a large tract of Federal lands—about six or seven million acres—and we wanted to abolish the old system, and get a better one for the government of the country, and we finally found it necessary to adopt the best system we could get" : Dane's letter to King ; *cf.* reference in previous note. The letter is also found in Spencer, *Hist. of U. S.*, ii., 208–9 ; *New York Tribune*, Feb. 28, 1855 ; Dunn, *Indiana*, 205–6 ; quotations also in Sato, *Land Question*, 107, and King, *Ohio*, 404–5.

[3] Dane to King, July 16, 1787 : "When I drew the ordinance,—which passed, a few words excepted, as I originally framed it," etc. Also statements of Dane in *Abridgment*, vii., 389 ; ix., App., 74–6 : King, *Ohio*, 405–9 ; and a letter to Webster, March 26, 1830 : *Mass. Hist. Soc. Proc., 1867–69*, 475–80.

in unmistakable terms whenever the subject arose, and without evidence to the contrary he should be credited with this important share of the work. But Dane may have done more. His statements convey the impression that his own judgment was employed to a large extent in selecting the matter from existing materials, in shaping it, and in arranging the general plan of the report. Carrington, we are told, "formed no part of it";[1] but he could hardly have maintained silence on so important a subject, and in a committee of which he was chairman. R. H. Lee and Melancthon Smith must have had much to do with the decision as to what should go into the report, since Dane states that these two agreed with him on some principles after the committee had met several times.[2] And yet, notwithstanding the doubt concerning the discussions which the committee may have had, the evidence at hand shows more or less clearly what they actually did. A view may thus be had of the scribe as he brought together into the report the previous results of congressional and State action and other material.

(c)— *The Report.*

The result of the committee's work is called " AN ORDINANCE FOR THE GOVERNMENT OF THE UNITED STATES NORTHWEST OF THE RIVER OHIO," and its opening paragraph is as follows : " *Be it ordained by the United States in Congress assembled,* that the said territory, for the purposes of temporary government, be one district ; subject, however, to be divided into two districts, as future circumstances may, in the opinion of Congress, make it expedient." The motion of Mr. Bland had conceived simply a large tract of territory divided into districts which should become States, but was indefinite regarding the organization of the whole. Likewise in the autumn of the same year, the resolution of

---

[1] Dane, *Abridgment*, ix., Appendix : King, *Ohio*, 408.
[2] Dane to King, July 16, 1787 : " We met several times and at last agreed on some principles ; at least Lee, Smith, and myself " : Bancroft, *Hist. of Formation of Const.*, ii., 431.

October 15 had declared " that it will be wise and necessary . . . to erect a district of the western territory
into a distinct government . . ." ;[1] but it contemplated
a single State. Nor was there in the law of 1784 any more
definite statement regarding the organization into one
whole of the several States outlined in it, to be dealt with
by Congress collectively. The ordinance reported April
26, 1787, was meant to cover the whole district of the
Northwest, as the amendments to the title show.[2] It appears that when the committee of which Johnson was
chairman had finished its work, there was a well formed
idea that a period of general control by Congress would be
necessary before any part could show itself ready for even
a temporary organization. The unity of the Northwest for
purposes of government was now clearly provided.

To the committee at its appointment was referred the
plan which had had its third reading on May 9.[3] It provided a complete temporary government, including governor, judges, and secretary, in the first stage, and a general
assembly composed of governor, council, and house, in the
second stage. The ordinance as a whole, with unimportant
changes in phraseology, was reproduced, but with these
differences : (1) Property and residence qualifications were
added for the office of governor, secretary, and judges ; (2)
The purpose of the division of the proposed district into
counties and townships was set forth more fully, and a
clause introduced limiting the part laid out to " the parts of
the district in which the Indian titles shall have been extinguished " ; (3) The clause granting a delegate with half
privilege was inserted ; (4) A long paragraph was introduced, defining how members of the proposed Legislative
Council of five should be appointed. The last was an idea
new to the history of congressional deliberation upon the
unorganized West, and should therefore be examined more

[1] *Journals of Congress,* iv., 296 ; Merriam, *Hist. of Ordinance,* 7, 8.
[2] Above, Sec. VIII.
[3] Above, Sects. VII. and VIII.

carefully. Apparently the only existing precedents [1] were
in Massachusetts and New Hampshire. The constitution
of the latter, however, was adopted in 1784, and differs
little from that of Massachusetts of four years before.[2]
This clause of the report provided that the members of
the executive council should be selected in this manner : at
a certain meeting of the elected representatives, there
should be nominated ten residents of the district, each
qualified by a freehold of five hundred acres ; these names
were to be sent to Congress, and out of them five council-
lors should be appointed.

Thus the bill which in May lacked little of becoming a
law, was changed and made a part of the present report.
This portion afforded a nucleus about which other matters
could be collected. Preceding this, and immediately following the statement of territorial extent, was arranged a
long paragraph, the purpose of which was to fix for the
western settlers the law of descent and conveyance of
estates. It was a large feature of the report, and in many
respects was quite new. In the first attempt at a plan for
disposing of the western lands, this subject was introduced ; [3] but if the provision had become a law, it would
have been different from that finally selected. Another
attempt to introduce this subject into legislation respecting
the West, and one in which, as has been seen,[4] Nathan

[1] *Mass. Const. of 1780*, Pt. 2, Chap. i., Sec. i., Art. iv. : "And in case
there shall not appear to be the full number of senators returned, elected by a
majority of votes for any district, the deficiency shall be supplied in the following manner, viz. : The members of the House of Representatives, and such
senators as shall be declared elected, shall take the names of such persons as
shall be found to have the highest number of votes in such district, and not
elected, amounting to twice the number of senators wanting, if there be so
many voted for, and out of these shall elect by ballot a number of senators
sufficient to fill up the vacancies in such district ; and in this manner all such
vacancies shall be filled up in every district of the commonwealth ; and in like
manner all vacancies in the senate, arising by death, removal out of the State,
or otherwise, shall be supplied as soon as may be after such vacancies shall happen " : Poore, *Charters*, 962–3 ; *Laws of Mass., 1780–1807*, i., 28.
[2] *Cf.*, New Hampshire Constitution of 1784 : Poore, *Charters*, 1285.
[3] Merriam, *Hist. of Ordinance*, 13.   [4] Above, Sec. VII.

Dane himself was interested, resulted in two paragraphs in the ordinance which Johnson reported in the autumn of 1786.[1] But they are brief, and are mere suggestions of what is fully treated in this last report. For this part Dane should be given most of the credit. There is reason to believe that he alone was concerned with it. First, he was a student of Massachusetts law, though certainly much less familiar with it in 1787 than after he had completed the ninth volume of his General Abridgment and Digest of American Law, forty-three years later. Secondly, he has assured the world many times that he took this part from the Massachusetts law.[2] Lastly, it is possible to turn to the very statutes[3] from which, there can be little doubt, the report was framed. They are found in the Massachusetts laws of 1784.[4] In February of this year a law was passed

---

[1] Printed in Merriam, *Hist. of Ordinance*, 19–20.

[2] The words of Dane at various places affirm this, so that it would be quite certain that this was the source, even though the laws themselves were not accessible. In his letter to Webster he states : "These titles occupy the first part of the Ordinance, not a page, evidently selected from the laws of Massachusetts, except it omits the double share of the oldest son" : *Mass. Hist. Soc. Proc., 1867–69*, 477. Further in the same letter : "In pages 389, 390, Sec. 3, Vol. 7th (of *Abridgment*), I mention the Ordinance of '87 was framed mainly from the laws of Massachusetts. This appears on the face of it ; meaning the titles to estates," etc. : *Ibid.*, 479. In the appendix to his *Abridgment*, ix., pp. 74–76, he also says : "The other description was selected mainly from the Constitution and Laws of Massachusetts, as any one may see who knows what American law was in '87 ; as I., Titles to property by will, by deed, by descent, and by delivery, cited verbatim in the seventh volume of this *Abridgment*, pages 389, 390" : King, *Ohio*, 407. "On the whole, if there be any praise or any blame in this ordinance, especially in the titles to property, and in the permanent parts, the most important of it belongs to Massachusetts" : *Ibid.*, 409.

[3] Mr. Merriam states that this part was taken from Massachusetts statutes of 1783, chap. 36 : *Hist. of Ordinance*, 25. No statute on this subject appears in the laws of 1783, in the edition of 1807. The confident statement of W. H. Smith, editor of the *St. Clair Papers*, that "the important clause on the descent and conveyance of real property is derived from the LI. article of the Constitution of Georgia of 1777" (Chicago *Dial*, ii., 295), is scarcely worth notice. *Cf.* the provision, in Poore, *Charters*, 383.

[4] Here follows this part of the committee's report, together with the corresponding passages in the Massachusetts laws :

"prescribing the manner of devising lands, tenements, and hereditaments," and in March one "directing the descent of

| REPORT OF THE COMMITTEE. | LAWS OF MASSACHUSETTS. |

Be it ordained by the authority aforesaid, That the estates both of resident and non-resident proprietors in the said territory dying intestate shall descend to and be distributed among their children and the descendants of a deceased child in equal parts ; the descendants of a deceased child or grandchild to take the share of their deceased parent in equal parts among them ; and where there shall be no children or descendants, then in equal parts to the next of kin, in equal degree ; and among collaterals, the children of a deceased brother or sister of the intestate shall have in equal parts among them, their deceased parents' share ; saving in all cases to the widow of the intestate her third part of the real estate for life, and where there shall be no children of the intestate, one-third part of the personal estate ; and this law relative to descents and dower shall remain in full force until altered by the legislature of the district. And until the governor and judges shall adopt laws, as hereinafter mentioned, estates in the said territory may be devised and bequeathed by wills in writing, signed and sealed by him or her in whom the estate may be (being of full age), and attested by three witnesses ; and real estates may be conveyed by lease or release, or bargain and sale, signed, sealed, and delivered by the person, being of full age, in whom the estate may be, and attested by two witnesses.

" That when any person shall die seized of lands, tenements or hereditaments, not by him devised, the same shall descend in equal shares to and among his children, and such as shall legally represent them (if any of them be dead) . . . ; and in every case where children shall inherit by representation it shall be in equal shares ; and where there are no children of the intestate, the inheritance shall descend equally to the next of kin in equal degree, and those who represent them, computing by the rules of the civil law—no person to be considered as a legal representative of collaterals beyond the degrees of brothers' and sisters' children ": Act, March 9, 1784, *Laws of Mass., 1780–1807,* i., 124–5.

" The surplusage, (if any there be) shall by the Judge of Probate, be decreed, one-third part to the widow of the deceased forever, unless the intestate died without issue, in which case she shall have one-half thereof forever" : *Ibid.,* 125.

" That every person lawfully seized of any lands, tenements, or hereditaments, . . . of the age of twenty-one years and upwards, . . . shall have power to give, dispose of and devise the same as well by last will and testament in writing as other ways. . . . That all devises and bequests of any lands or tenements shall be in writing, and signed by the party so devising the same . . . , and shall be attested and subscribed in the presence of the said devisor, by three or more credible witnesses . . ." : Act, Feb. 6, 1784, *Laws of Mass., 1780–1807,* i., 109–10.

intestate estates." Considerably more than a century before this, however, the former had been the subject of provincial legislation in Massachusetts,[1] and parts of the latter had been touched upon in 1647, 1692, 1710, 1719, and 1734.[2] As it it stood in 1787, the law of March 9, 1784, had not been changed. It provided for the descent of property to children or their representatives in equal parts; but there was this exception to the equality of inheritance by the children : the eldest son received two shares. Even this precedence did not long remain a part of the Massachusetts law ; but it was there when Dane incorporated the general principles of the law into the committee's report, and had he been less alive to the fact that republican institutions do not favor distinctions between oldest and younger or between males and females, he might have allowed this reminder of feudalism to be reported to Congress. Had he done so, doubtless some one else would have gained the credit of striking out this inequality. Dane, however, purposely omitted this and should have the credit of the intention.[3] Thus did the law regarding the descent of property become purely republican. By the custom known as gavelkind, which had been proposed three years before in this connection,[4] the sons inherited alike, but the daughters were not recognized as

---

The law of conveyance is not so clear a case as the law of descent. However the above excerpt from the Massachusetts laws in force at the time the report was made, on the subject of conveyance, seems to be the nearest approximation to the report among them. Some of Dane's references to the matter almost imply that a part of this may have come from other laws. This Massachusetts statute on the law of conveyance of estates appears to be remodeled from a provincial statute of the year 1692. *Cf.*, *Province Laws*, 1692-3, Chap. 14 : *Acts and Resolves of the Prov.*, i., 43-45 ; *Laws of Mass.*, 1780-1807, ii., 969-70.

[1] 1652 : *Laws of Mass.*, 1780-1807, ii., 962-3.

[2] *Ibid.*, ii., 964-5, 969-70, 993, 1000, 1001, 1009-10 ; *Acts and Resolves of the Prov.*, i., 43-5, 652 ; ii., 738-9.

[3] " These titles .   .   . evidently selected from the laws of Massachusetts, except it omits the double share of the oldest son.   .   .   . I believe these were the first titles to property, completely republican, in Federal America ; being in no part whatever feudal or monarchical " : *Letter to Webster*, March 26, 1830, in *Mass. Hist. Soc. Proc.*, 1867-69, 477.

[4] Merriam, *Hist. of Ordinance*, 13.

equal with the sons in respect to rights.[1]   In the report of
September, 1786, the equality of the sons and daughters
was made very specific: " Male and female in equal
parts."

This part of the report, therefore, included the law regarding title to property by descent, by will, by deed, and by
delivery.   An addition was made providing that change of
estates under this law should be properly recorded within a
year after the establishment of the necessary civil function-
aries, and also a final stipulation that the French law in
force among the Illinois and Mississippi villages, as far as it
regulated the descent and conveyance of property, should
not be supplanted by the law in the proposed ordinance.

Nor was this all the report.   The law governing property
and the scheme of government were important.   But the
officers would be temporary; and while the part concerning
property was intended to remain a permanent heritage of
the people with whom it might gain a foothold, yet even
this does not rank with those fundamental principles according to which the people had come to interpret their constitutions and to administer their laws.   It might well have
been seen that these must be guaranteed to all new States,
if they and the Confederation desired no uncertainty in
their relations.   The committee who formed the report of
March 1, 1784, did not fail to provide " principles " for both
temporary and permanent governments, and however the
action may have been brought about, it is well that the
present committee embodied in their report a large measure
of the results of State and Federal experience.   To the two
parts of their report already mentioned, the committee
added five articles and introduced them by the following
paragraph :

" And for extending to all parties [2] of the Confederacy
the fundamental principles of civil and religious liberty,

[1] Wharton, *Law Lexicon* (1883), 360-1 ; Bouvier, *Law Dictionary* (1883),
706.
[2] Merriam, *Hist. of Ordinance*, 29; Mr. Force has " parts " : *St. Clair Papers*,
ii., 616, and *Life of Cutler*, ii., 423.

which form the basis whereon these republics, their laws and Constitutions are erected ; to fix and establish those principles as the basis of all laws, constitutions, and governments which forever hereafter shall be formed in the said territory⊙to provide also for the establishment of States and permanent government therein, and for their admission to a share in the Federal Councils on an equal footing with the original States, at as early periods as may be consistent with the general interest : It is hereby ordained and declared by the authority aforesaid, that the following articles shall be considered as articles of compact between the original States and the people and States in the said territory and forever remain unalterable, unless by common consent." The idea of a compact between the new States and the original thirteen first appeared in the report of March 1, 1784 ; and from that, or from the act as it passed April 23, 1784, the idea was transferred to the present report.[1]

The source of these articles and the occasion of their introduction into the Ordinance of 1787 has caused much controversy. A careful consideration of the sources is, therefore, not in vain, if any results can thereby be obtained. How the articles came into the report will be noticed later.[2]

The first article is: " No person demeaning himself in a peaceable and orderly manner, shall ever be molested on account of his mode of worship or religious sentiments, in the said territory." After a careful comparison of the pharaseology of the corresponding clauses in the constitutions of the different States, all the evidence points to sections two and twelve of the Declaration of Rights in the Massachusetts Constitution of 1780.[3] The second article

---

[1] Writers seem to have traced the idea of a compact no further back than the report of Jefferson.

[2] Below, Sec. IX. (d).

[3] Compare these excerpts from the constitutions of the States :

(a) Massachusetts, Const. of 1780. Sects. 2 and 3 : " And every denomination of christians demeaning themselves peaceably and as good subjects of the com-

summarized those principles of the common law that secure personal liberty.   The first provision was that inhabitants should always have the benefits of the writ of *habeas corpus* and trial by jury, and the language is identical with that used in the draft of the previous autumn.'   Proportionate representation in the legislature and judicial proceeding according to the common law were also provided.   The former secured permanently to the territory what was provided in their temporary organization ; the latter was everywhere admitted.   It further provided : " All persons shall be bailable unless for capital offenses, where the proof shall be evident or the presumption great; all fines shall be moderate, and no cruel or unusual punishments shall be inflicted."   The provisions in the various constitutions concerning bail, fines, and punishments are very similar, and it

---

monwealth, shall be equally under the protection of the laws.   And no subject shall be hurt, molested, or restrained, in his person, liberty, or estate, for worshiping God in the manner and season most agreeable to the dictates of his own conscience, or for his religious profession or sentiments. . . ."   Poore, *Charters*, 957–3.

(b) Virginia, Bill of Rights, 1776, Sec. 16 : " And . . . all men are equally entitled to the free exercise of religion according to the dictates of conscience." Poore, *Charters*, 1909.

(c) Pennsylvania, Const. of 1776, Declaration of Rights, Sec. 2 : " Nor can any man, who acknowledges the being of a God, be justly deprived or abridged of any civil right as a citizen, on account of his religious sentiments or peculiar mode of worship."   Poore, *Charters*, 1541.

(d) Maryland, Const. of 1776, Declaration of Rights, Sec. 33 : " Wherefore no person ought by any law to be molested in his person or estate, on account of his religious persuasion, or profession, or for his religious practice." Poore, *Charters*, 819.

(e) Georgia, Const. of 1777, lvi. : " All persons whatever shall have the free exercise of their religion."   Poore, *Charters*, 383.

It is thought unnecessary to quote from the New Hampshire Constitution of 1784, since it is largely a reproduction of the Massachusetts Constitution of 1780.   The editor of the *St. Clair Papers* does not seem to be aware of this when he observes that " The language of the New Hampshire Constitution of 1784, on the same subject, is strikingly like that of the Ordinance" : Chicago *Dial*, ii., 296, April, 1882.   Certainly this is true ; but Art. 5 of the Bill of Rights in the New Hampshire Constitution of 1784 is the same as Art. 2 of the Declaration of Rights in the Massachusetts Constitution of 1780.   *Cf.* Poore, *Charters*, 957, 1281.

' *Cf.* the provision : Merriam, *Hist. of Ordinance*, 19.

cannot be said which was the model, if any. None, however, has more claim than the Massachusetts constitution.[1] Likewise the next provision, which was that a man should not be deprived of liberty or property except by the judgment of his peers or the law of the land, and that compensation should be given for property or services required, is found to be similar in the several constitutions.[2] It looks back to the

[1] Compare the following :

(a) Massachusetts, Const. of 1780, Declaration of Rights, Sec. 26 : "No magistrate or court of laws shall demand excessive bail or sureties, impose excessive fines, or inflict cruel or unusual punishments." Poore, *Charters*, 959.

(b) Virginia, Const. of 1776, Bill of Rights, Sec. 9 : "That excessive bail ought not to be required, nor excessive fines imposed, nor cruel or unusual punishments inflicted." Poore, *Charters*, 1909.

(c) Maryland, Const. of 1776, Declaration of Rights, Sec. 22 : "That excessive bail ought not to be required, nor excessive fines imposed, nor cruel or unusual punishments inflicted, by the courts of law." Poore, *Charters*, 818.

(d) North Carolina, Const. of 1776, Declaration of Rights, Sec. 10 : "That excessive bail should not be required, nor excessive fines imposed, nor cruel or unusual punishment inflicted." Poore, *Charters*, 1409.

(e) Georgia, Const. of 1777, lix. : "Excessive fines shall not be levied, nor excessive bail demanded." Poore, *Charters*, 383.

(f) Connecticut, Const. of 1776, Part 4 : "And that no man's person shall be restrained or imprisoned by any authority whatsoever, before the law hath sentenced him thereunto, if he can and will give sufficient Security, Bail, or Mainprize, for his Appearance and good Behavior in the meantime, unless it be for Capital Crimes, Contempt in open court. . . ." Poore, *Charters*, 258.

The last has been cited as "closely parallel" to the clause concerning bail in the report : Merriam, *Hist. of Ordinance*, 30. But the same can be as truly said for similar provisions in other constitutions. With regard to the part of Article II. requiring moderate fines and no unusual punishments, Mr. Merriam thinks that the language was probably suggested by the Virginia Bill of Rights ("b," quoted above) : *Hist. of Ordinance*, 30, 31. Plainly it is difficult to do more than state a probability. Between the "*ought not to be required*" of the constitutions of Maryland and Virginia, the "*should not be required*" of that of North Carolina, and the "*shall demand*" and "*shall not be demanded*" in the constitutions of Massachusetts and Georgia, only opinions can be entertained.

[2] The words of the report were : "No man shall be deprived of his liberty or property, but by the judgment of his peers or the law of the land ; and should the public exigencies make it necessary for the common preservation, to take any one's property, or to demand his particular service, full compensation shall be made for the same." *Cf.* the clauses in the constitutions :

(a) Massachusetts, Const. of 1780, Declaration of Rights, Sects. 10 and 12 : "And no subject shall be arrested, imprisoned, despoiled, or deprived of his

words of the Magna Charta : " No freeman shall be taken, or imprisoned, or disseized, or outlawed, or banished, . . . unless by the lawful judgment of his peers, or by the law of the land." A comparison shows that it is found as well in the Massachusetts constitution as in any other.

The next part of this same article is the provision relating to private contracts. Now for the first time, interference

property, immunities, or privileges, but out of the protection of the law, exiled or deprived of his life, liberty, or estate, but by the judgment of his peers or the law of the land." " But no part of the property of any individual can with justice, be taken from him, or applied to public uses, without his own consent or that of the representative body of the people. . . . And whenever the public exigencies require that the property of any individual should be appropriated to public uses, he shall receive a reasonable compensation therefor. He is obliged . . . to give his personal service or an equivalent, when necessary." Poore, *Charters*, 958.

(b) Virginia, Const. of 1776, Bill of Rights, Sects. 6 and 8 : " That no man be deprived of his liberty, except by the law of the land or the judgment of his peers." " And that all men having sufficient evidence of permanent common interest with, and attachment to, the community, have the right of suffrage, and cannot be taxed or deprived of their property for public uses, without their own consent or that of their representatives so elected." Poore, *Charters*, 1909.

(c) Pennsylvania, Const. of 1776, Declaration of Rights, Sects. 8 and 9 : " That every member of society hath a right to be protected in the enjoyment of life, liberty, and property, and therefore is bound to contribute his proportion towards the expense of that protection, and yield his personal service when necessary, or an equivalent thereto : But no part of a man's property can be justly taken from him, or applied to public uses, without his own consent, or that of his legal representatives. Nor can any man be justly deprived of his liberty, except by the laws of the land, or the judgment of his peers." Poore, *Charters*, 1541-2.

(d) Maryland, Const. of 1776, Declaration of Rights, Sec. 21 : " That no freeman ought to be taken, or imprisoned, or disseized of his freehold, liberties, or privileges, or outlawed or exiled, or in any manner destroyed, or deprived of his life, liberty, or property, but by the judgment of his peers, or by the law of the land." Poore, *Charters*, 818.

(e) North Carolina, Const. of 1776, Declaration of Rights, Sec. 12 : " That no freeman ought to be taken, imprisoned, or disseized of his freehold, liberties, or privileges, or outlawed or exiled, or in any manner destroyed, or deprived of his life, liberty, or property, but by the law of the land. Poore, *Charters*, 1410

The constitutions of Massachusetts and Pennsylvania seem to be the only ones which speak of the government requiring " personal service." Mr. Merriam is very positive that " Virginia and Massachusetts together contributed " these provisions : *Hist. of Ordinance*, 31.

with them is forbidden by law, except where they are illegal. It has, therefore, become a matter of some interest to know who first suggested it. The committee reported: "And in the just preservation of rights and property, it is understood and declared, that no law ought ever to be made or have force in the said territory, that shall in any manner whatever, interfere with or affect private contracts or engagements, *bona fide*, and without fraud, previously formed." Dane claimed to have originated this,[1] and doubtless he did frame it in his own words and put it in its place in the report. It could not be found elsewhere. But he may not have been the first to speak of it. The evidence deduced by Dr. Bancroft to show that R. H. Lee had thought of this earlier in the same year, prevents the view that Mr. Dane claimed originality as to idea.[2] The purpose of the measure was understood to refer to the abuses of paper money.[3]

There were two subjects in the third article: encouragement to morality and education, and preservation of good faith in dealing with Indians. The part referring to the former was brief, but it has attracted more attention, perhaps, than any other part of the committee's report. "Institutions for the promotion of religion, morality, schools and the means of education shall forever be encouraged, and all persons, while young, shall be taught some useful occupation." The authorship of this provision, together with that of the article on slavery, which was added later, has been the centre of interest in the discussion of the

---

[1] *Abridgment*, ix., Appendix: "As to matter, he [Dane] furnished the provision respecting impairing contracts, and the Indian security, and some other smaller matters": King, *Ohio*, 409. *Cf.* Dane to Webster, March 26, 1830: "I have never claimed *originality* except in regard to the clause against impairing contracts, and perhaps the *Indian* article": *Mass. Hist. Soc. Proc., 1867–69,* 479.

[2] Dr. Bancroft, *Hist. of U. S.* (Fin. Rev.), vi., 288, and *Hist. of Formation of Const.*, ii., 113, citing Lee to George Mason, May 15, 1787, *Life of R. H. Lee*, ii., 71–73; and also Sparks, *Letters to Washington*, iv., 174. *Cf.* Stone, *Ordinance of 1787*, in *Penn. Mag. of Hist. and Biog.*, xiii., 337–8; Merriam, *Hist. of Ordinance*, 31–2.

[3] Otto to Mortmain, July 20, 1787: Bancroft, *Hist. of Formation of Const.*, ii., 432.

Ordinance of 1787. An analysis shows that the occasion of its introduction into the report is the doubtful part of the matter, rather than who put it in or framed it. For there is nothing to show that Mr. Dane was not its author, and there is much reason to believe that he was. There is enough in the constitution of Massachusetts to have suggested the form of the provision.[1] Mr. Dane did not claim originality in regard to this, but what he did say has not been understood on account of his obscure style. His language, indeed, has misled some of the best writers on the subject.[2] He declared that he took the provision from the

---

[1] In the Declaration of Rights, Sec. 3, there occurs the following : "As the happiness of a people and the good order and preservation of civil government essentially depend upon piety, religion, and morality, and as these cannot be generally diffused through a community but by the institution of the public worship of God, and of public instructions in piety, religion, and morality : therefore, to promote their happiness and to secure the good order and preservation of this government," etc. : Poore, *Charters*, 957. And Chapter v. of the Constitution, entitled " Encouragement to Literature," etc., is as follows : " Wisdom and knowledge, as well as virtue, diffused generally among the body of the people, being necessary for the preservation of their rights and liberties ; and as these depend on spreading the opportunities and advantages of education in the various parts of the country, and among the different orders of the people, it shall be the duty of legislatures and magistrates in all future periods of this commonweath, to cherish the interests of literature and the sciences, and all seminaries of them," etc.

[2] One of Mr. Dane's statements is : " I have never claimed *originality*, except in regard to the clause against impairing contracts, and perhaps the Indian article, part of the third article, including, also, religion, morality, knowledge, schools, etc." : Letter to Webster, *Mass. Hist. Soc. Proc., 1867-69*, 479. By this he must mean, " and perhaps the Indian article, a part of the third article, which includes, also, religion, morality," etc. Again, he states in his *Abridgment*, ix., Appendix : " The other description was selected mainly from the constitution and laws of Massachusetts . . . as I., Titles to property," etc. " II., All the fundamental, perpetual articles of compact (except as below)—1st, securing forever religious liberty ; 2d, the essential parts of a bill of rights declaring that ' religion, morality, and knowledge, being necessary to good government and the happiness of mankind, schools and the means of education shall forever be encouraged.' These selections from the code of Massachusetts," etc. : King, *Ohio*, 407. Mr. Dane evidently meant to say that he selected this provision concerning morality and education from the Massachusetts law ; and there is no reason to interpret it otherwise. Dr. Poole and Mr. Stone have both misunderstood this : *Dr. Cutler and the Ordinance of 1787*, in *N. A. Rev.*, vol. cxxii., pp. 259-60 ; *Penn. Mag. of Hist. and Biog.*, xiii., 338.

5

Massachusetts code. A possible motive for introducing this provision will be considered elsewhere.

The latter part of the third article, which secured to the Indians fair treatment, property rights, liberty, and legislation in their behalf, Dane felt was his own. Not that the idea was new, perhaps, for it was not. Much had been said upon the subject since Roger Williams championed the cause of the Indians. But Dane thought that he had contributed this much without copying it from any particular place.[1]

Article iv. embodied all but one of the seven principles in the law of 1784, together with the motion of Grayson regarding the navigation of the tributaries of the Mississippi and St. Lawrence.[2] No material change was made in these, but a clause was added to the effect that the taxes apportioned to a new State by Congress should be levied by its legislature. The sixth principle of the law of 1784 was reserved for Article v. The words of the provision for free navigation were not changed.[3]

The motion of Grayson to divide the Northwest into five States, by drawing a parallel at the southern point of Lake Michigan and allowing two States above and three below,[4] was the basis for the division outlined in the fifth article. It provided for a division into "not less than three nor more than five states," which had been agreed upon during the previous summer.[5] The meridian of the mouth of the Wabash, however, was changed to the meridian of "Post Vincent's," thus allowing the Wabash to be a boundary to some extent. With the meridian at the mouth of the Great Miami there would thus be formed three States. It was

---

[1] For other views and general reference to the subject, see *St. Clair Papers*, i., 131 ; Stone, *Penn. Mag. of Hist. and Biog.*, xiii., 337 ; Merriam, *Hist. of Ordinance*, 33 ; Dunn, *Indiana*, 207-8 ; King, *Ohio*, 187-8 ; Williams, *Arthur St. Clair and the Ordinance of 1787*, in *Mag. West. Hist.*, i., 61.

[2] Above, Sec. VI.

[3] Merriam, *Hist. of Ordinance*, 34, citing *Journals of Congress*, iv., 637-8.

[4] Above, Sec. VI.

[5] Above, Sec. VI.

further provided that if Congress found it expedient, one or two States might be formed north of the parallel at the southern extreme of Lake Michigan. These boundaries were to become " fixed and established " as soon as Virginia should " alter her act of cession and authorize the same." [1] In this article, also, a final conclusion was reached with regard to requirement for admission. The colony of soldiers which Pickering's draft conceived was to arrive at statehood at one bound and gain forthwith admission to Congress by its delegates.[2] Bland's ordinance would have turned such aspirations to despair by causing the territory to wait until it should have 20,000 male inhabitants.[3] The provision in the draft reported by Jefferson, that the State to be admitted must have a population equal to that of the least numerous of the thirteen original States, remained the requirement until the changes in the committee during the summer and autumn of 1786. After the appointment of new members at that time, the prejudice against the admission of new States found expression in a higher requirement : that a new State must have a population equal to one thirteenth of the number in the Confederacy. Better counsels, or rather the vote of Congress, prevailed, and this requirement was struck out. Now it was provided that " whenever any of the said States shall have 60,000 free inhabitants therein, such State shall be admitted, by its delegates, into the Congress of the United States, on an equal footing with the original States in all respects whatever, and shall be at liberty to form a permanent constitution and State government."

The sixth principle completed the article. Many times since the resolution of Congress of October 10, 1780, had declared that ceded territory should be " formed into distinct republican States," had the republican character of future States been asserted. The following paragraph, de-

---

[1] Act of Virginia ratifying the change, Dec. 30, 1788 : Hening, *Statutes*, xii., 780-1.

[2] Above, Sec. II.

[3] Above, Sec. II.

claring this and modifying the requirement for admission [1]
as a hard and fast rule, completed the report of the committee : " *Provided*, the constitution and government so to be
formed shall be republican, and in conformity to the principles stated in these articles, and so far as it can be consistent
with the general interest of the confederacy, such admission
shall be allowed at an earlier period, and when there may
be a less number of free inhabitants in the State than 60,000."

The idea of new colonies to the westward of the old thirteen existed long before the colonies severed the tie which
bound them to the mother country ; but it is surprising
that less than four months after the famous Fourth of July
on which that separation was proclaimed the Maryland convention made the declaration that such lands as were
conquered by the united strength of the colonies " ought to
be considered as a common stock to be parcelled out at
proper times into convenient, free, and independent governments." [2] This was before there was any union into
which new States might be received. But as soon as there
was developed a pretty definite idea of a union of the colonies under one government, it was declared that these new
organizations which might be formed from the unsettled
West should be republican, and that they should come into
the league of States to enjoy the common benefits and bear
the common burdens. In the final article of the report
these ideas were embodied.

(d)—*The Influence of Manasseh Cutler.*

Thus was the report of the committee finished. An attempt has been made to discover, as far as the evidence
allows, whence it was drawn. It has appeared that the committee or their draughtsman had at hand the previous ordi-

---

[1] Even with a requirement for 60,000 population the Northeast was not
satisfied. Dane said in his letter to King that he thought the requirement
too small. He consoled himself with the thought that perhaps the new State
first admitted would adopt eastern politics.

[2] Resolve of the Maryland Convention, Oct. 30, 1776: *Amer. Archives*, Fifth
Series, iii., 134.

nances, the motions of Grayson, the Code of Massachusetts, and perhaps the constitutions or laws of other States. Motives of action have not been discovered. It has not been shown why particular provisions should have been selected rather than others, or selected at all, unless it has appeared that Mr. Dane himself had a choice. One influence brought to bear upon the committee needs to be considered in this connection. The agent of the Ohio Company had not yet completed his purchase, and was present with Congress during a portion of the time probably occupied by the committee in preparing their report. What had Manasseh Cutler been doing on that Monday and Tuesday, July 9 and 10? During the forenoon of the preceding Friday Dr. Cutler delivered his letters to Congressmen, prepared his petition for land purchase, and submitted it.[1] He took dinner with Mr. Dane, who was a member of the committee on purchase of land and afterwards of the one on the ordinance; but it will be noticed that Mr. Dane was not the only one with whom he dined. Dane and the Comptroller of the Board of Treasury lived together, Dr. Cutler tells us in his *Journal*, and owing to the fact that Cutler had no great reverence for Dane as a man, it is likely that he dined quite as much with the Comptroller of the Board as with Dane. Cutler spent the evening with several members of Congress, and on Saturday[2] met Thomas Hutchins, Geographer to the United States, and consulted him on location. No one has yet ascertained that Cutler came to Congress with a single thought as to the western government; but if he did have such a thought, or was in any wise especially interested in that subject, Monday was the time he would have shown it. Early that morning he sought Mr. Hutchins and obtained full information of the western country and advice to locate on the Muskingum. He left Mr. Hutchins only long enough to wait on the land committee before Congress opened, and then returned to spend the remainder of the forenoon with the man who could give him the best

---

[1] Cutler's Diary, July 6 : *Life of Cutler*, i., 230.
[2] Cutler's Diary, July 7 . *Life of Cutler*, i., 230.

information regarding the West.¹   After dining with some
clergymen, the Doctor reluctantly left this sociable company
to attend the land committee and settle terms of contract,
but the parties "were so wide apart " that there appeared
"little prospect of closing a contract." ²   After this the ob-
servant scientist took a lively interest in the curious things
to be seen in the halls where the Federal legislators met.
Members of the committee showed him about the building,
and he has left in his *Journal* ³ a thorough description of
what was then the council-chamber of the Confederacy.
After again consulting Hutchins he spent the evening with
Dr. Holton and other members of Congress in the same
quarter of the city.   Thus ended the day on which the
ordinance was referred to the committee, and as far as it
appears, Dr. Cutler may not have been aware that the subject had been revived.   The next morning he again conferred with the committee on land and visited Columbia
College.⁴   That day he dined with the president and secretary of the Board of Treasury.   He does not state what
hour this was, but he tells us that Duer, the secretary, lived
in the style of a nobleman,⁵ and doubtless it was a fashion-
able hour.   The next entry in his *Journal* is the important
one as regards the report of the committee given the following day.   He writes: "As Congress was now engaged in
settling the form of government for the Federal Territory,
for which a bill had been prepared, and a copy sent to me
with leave to make remarks and propose amendments, and
which I had taken the liberty to remark upon and to propose several amendments, I thought this the most favorable
opportunity to go on to Philadelphia.   Accordingly after I
had returned the bill with my observations, I set out at seven
o'clock and crossed North River to Paulus Hook." ⁶   When

¹ Cutler's Diary, July 9 : *Life of Cutler*, i., 236.
² Cutler's Diary, July 9 : *Life of Cutler*, i., 237.
³ Cutler's Diary, July 9 : *Life of Cutler*, i., 237–8.
⁴ Cutler's Diary, July 10 :, *Life of Cutler*, i., 239.
⁵ Cutler's Diary, July 10 : *Life of Cutler*, i., 240–1.
⁶ Cutler's Diary, July 10 : *Life of Cutler*, i., 242.

Cutler returned over a week later he found in the ordinance, passed in the meantime, the amendments he had suggested, except one.[1]   What they were is the problem.

What ordinance was handed to Dr. Cutler? Was it the one prepared in the spring relating to temporary government, or was it one drawn by the committee of July 9? The expression of Dr. Cutler on seeing the ordinance after it had passed was, " It is in a degree new-modeled."[2]   With nothing to the contrary, this would be strong ground for thinking that when he saw the ordinance on July 10, the committee having it in charge had not prepared their report.[3] On the other hand, the committee had been appointed Monday, and it would be strange if they should let the rest of that day and nearly all of Tuesday pass before beginning their work. The impression left by Dr. Cutler's words is that it was just before he left the city that he returned the ordinance, or " bill," as he calls it. " Accordingly, after I had returned the bill with my observations, I set out at seven o'clock." At least the day was far gone. It seems rather more probable, therefore, that some work had been done on the report. The land purchase was an important matter, and Dane implies in his letter to Rufus King, that it had a material effect upon the quality of the committee's report.[4] If they had anything better than the draft of the spring, it is likely that they submitted it to Cutler. If they had a draft in any measure prepared, what did it contain ? In all probability it was made up of those parts which it would have received without any outside influence. Dane would do on one committee what he did on another, perhaps; and the law governing the descent and conveyance of property would probably have become a part of the report without Dr. Cutler's assistance. Whatever was brought together from the old ordinances and from separate enactments of Congress, might have been expected to appear in the report.

---

[1] Cutler's Diary, July 19 : *Life of Cutler*, i., 293.
[2] Cutler's Diary, July 19 : *Life of Cutler*. i., 293.
[3] *Cf.* Merriam, *Hist. of Ordinance*, 40.
[4] Bancroft, *Hist. of Formation of Const.*, ii., 431.

This would embrace the fourth and fifth articles. Whatever was due to Cutler seems likely to be contained in the first three articles. He can hardly have suggested all of these. No doubt parts of them were already in the report, and we may conclude from the fact that it was "new-modeled" when Cutler afterwards saw it, that it was presented to him in a different form. Indeed, in this connection there would be no improbability in supposing a suggestion by Dr. Cutler as to an arrangement of the parts. When he saw the ordinance on his return, Cutler wrote also: "The amendments I proposed have all been made except one, and that is better qualified." [1] Does not his language imply several amendments or changes? Would he have written that the amendments had "all" been made except one, if there had been but two or three?

Among the files of Ohio documents that were in the Cutler family, was the Ordinance of 1787 on a printed sheet, and "on the margin was written that Mr. Dane requested Dr. Cutler to suggest such provisions as he deemed advisable, and that at Dr. Cutler's instance was inserted what relates to religion, education, and slavery." [2] As far as there is nothing to the contrary this will be allowed, and the following would seem to have been the proceeding:—Dane having been intrusted by the committee with the work of drawing up the ordinance, submitted to Cutler what he had prepared. With his suggestions Dane returned to his task, remodeled the draft, and made use of all the suggestions except one, or possibly two. One item omitted is mentioned in Dr. Cutler's Journal, and had reference to taxation.

---

[1] Cutler's Diary, July 19 : *Life of Cutler*, i., 293.

[2] Dr. Poole in the *No. Am. Rev.*, vol. 122, p. 261, citing a letter of Dr. Joseph Torrey to Judge Ephraim Cutler, Jan. 30, 1847, which relates that he saw this document. *Cf. Life of Cutler*, i., 343. Because of the fact that the Ohio Company and their agent were all the while asking for a private contract, and since this purchase, when finally made, was really a private contract on a large scale, some have drawn the inference that it was at Dr. Cutler's instance that Dane inserted the provision with regard to the obligation of contracts : W. P. Cutler, *Private Contract Provision in Ordinance of 1787*, in *Mag. Amer. Hist.*, xiii., 483-6.

The other is the anti-slavery provision.[1]   To what extent the arrangement of the report was due to Cutler does not appear, nor will it probably be known how far the embodiment of the principles from bills of rights was occasioned by his suggestions.

[1] Below, Sec. X. (b).

X.

THE REPORT BEFORE CONGRESS.

(a)—*The Minor Amendments.*

On Wednesday, July 11, the report of the committee was submitted to Congress. Thursday, at its second reading, it was variously altered. In the case of minor changes in wording, it is not known who moved the amendments; but the different handwritings show who were some of those most interested in the ordinance. Two additions were made to the part which regulated descent and conveyance of property, and both are in the handwriting of Grayson, the acting president of Congress.[1] The first added after the clause providing that "among collaterals the children of a deceased brother or sister of the intestate shall have in equal parts among them their deceased parents' share," "*and there shall in no case be a distinction between kindred of the whole and half blood.*" The other touched the clause referring to the French settlers. Instead of reading, "saving, however, to the inhabitants of Kaskaskia and Post Vincent, their laws and customs now in force among them, relative to the descent and conveyance of property," it was made to read, "saving however to the French and Canadian *inhabitants and other settlers of the Kaskaskias, St. Vincents, and the neighboring villages who have heretofore professed themselves citizens of Virginia,* their laws and customs now in force among them," etc. The clause, "where there shall be no children of the intestate," also was struck out. An important change

---

[1] Merriam, *Hist. of Ordinance*, 25-6 ; Force, *Hist. of Ordinance : St. Clair Papers*, ii., 613, and *Life of Cutler*, ii., 420.

of words in the part relating to temporary government [1] was made in the hand of Charles Thompson, Secretary of Congress, as were also the insertion of the definite article several times in Article v.,[2] and an amendment to Article iii.[3] The first clause of the latter was reported by the committee, " Institutions for the promotion of religion, morality, schools and the means of education shall forever be encouraged, and all persons while young shall be taught some useful occupation." The first five words and the last clause were struck out, and a new clause inserted, so that the sentence became, " Religion, morality, and knowledge being necessary to good government and the happiness of mankind, schools and the means of education shall forever be encouraged." It was also thought better to speak of Virginia consenting to a change of boundaries in the proposed States, rather than authorizing it, and the president made the change.[4]

(b)— *The Anti-slavery Amendment.*

It has been noted [5] that Dr. Cutler is claimed to have suggested to Dane, among other amendments, a provision regarding slavery ; but it did not appear in the draft as submitted to Congress. The question first arises, was this really among the amendments that Cutler proposed ? The direct evidence to support the view that it was, has been already mentioned. To favor this is the fact that in the first move on the part of the soldiers to frame a plan for a new State, viz., that by Pickering, Putnam, and others, in 1783,[6] a positive slavery prohibition was included. It can-

---

[1] Merriam, *Hist. of Ordinance*, 27 ; Force, *Hist. of Ordinance : St. Clair Papers*, ii., 614, and *Life of Cutler*, ii., 421.

[2] Merriam, *Hist. of Ordinance*, 34 ; Force, *Hist. of Ordinance : St. Clair Papers*, ii., 617, and *Life of Cutler*, ii., 426.

[3] Merriam, *Hist. of Ordinance*, 32 ; Force, *Hist. of Ordinance: St. Clair Papers*, ii., 616, and *Life of Cutler*, ii., 424.

[4] Merriam, *Hist. of Ordinance*, 34 ; Force, *Hist. of Ordinance : St. Clair Papers*, ii., 617, and *Life of Cutler*, ii., 426.

[5] Above, Sec. IX. (d).

[6] Above, Sec. II. (a).

not be doubted, therefore, that among the officers of the
army who were interested in the West, anti-slavery sentiment prevailed.   Putnam was interested in the Ohio-Com-
pany purchase also, just as he had before taken a prominent
part in the plan and the petition of 1783.   Dr. Cutler must
have been aware of this sentiment, and if it was his endeav-
or to suit the associators of the company, he would have
mentioned this, along with other things, as desirable amendments.   If, on the other hand, Dr. Cutler consulted his own
opinion in the matter, it is not so certain that he would
have cared much for an anti-slavery clause.   His later
history at least does not show that he was a very ardent
champion of that cause.   He was one of the representatives
from Massachusetts in the eighth Congress; and when it
was moved, on January 18, 1805, to begin on the fourth of
July of that year to emancipate gradually the slaves within
the national District, Manasseh Cutler voted against the
measure.[1]   Twice in the consideration of this question did
he oppose an anti-slavery move.   He may have had special
reasons for thus recording his vote; but, to say the least, it
does not show on his part any great anxiety in the cause of
anti-slavery.

   Granted, however, that he indicated to Dane a desire to
have the provision placed in the ordinance, why did not Dane
insert it in the report of the committee ?   To this question
there is no more direct answer anywhere than Dane himself
makes in his letter to Rufus King, dated the next Monday.
His words are these: " When I drew the ordinance which
passed (a few words excepted) as I originally formed it, I had
no idea the states would agree to the sixth article, prohibit-
ing slavery, as only Massachusetts, of the eastern states,
was present, and therefore omitted it in the draft."[2]   It certainly did appear that the southern States had things much
their own way in matters where negative votes would
express their sentiments.   Of the northern States there were

---

[1] *Annals of Congress*, 8th Cong., 2d Sess., 1804-5, p. 995 ; Benton, *Debates,*
iii., 313.

[2] Bancroft, *Hist. of Formation of Const.*, ii., 431 ; *Life of Cutler,* i., 372.

present, on July 4, New York, Massachusetts, and New
Jersey; of the southern States, Virginia, North and South
Carolina, and Georgia.' Delaware soon appeared; and
surely, if this was the constitution of Congress when Dane
was deliberating whether or not to add the amendment relative to slavery, it is no wonder that he hesitated. The South
had not been accustomed to oppose slavery when the subject
arose in Congress, and Dane could not have been expected
to think they would readily fall in with the measure.

At any rate, the proposition did not appear in the report,
and not until Congress had fairly finished consideration of
the ordinance, was the part relating to slavery brought
forward. Continuing in the letter above quoted, Dane
wrote: "but, finding the House favorably disposed on this
subject, after we had completed the other parts, I moved the
article, which was agreed to without opposition." He proposed that the following, which is largely in the words of the
amended motion of King,² should be added as a final article:
"There shall be neither slavery nor involuntary servitude in
the said territory, otherwise than in the punishment of
crimes, whereof the party shall have been duly convicted:
Provided always, That any person escaping into the same,
from whom labor or service is lawfully claimed in any one of
the original States, such fugitive may be lawfully reclaimed
and conveyed to the person claiming his or her labor or
service."

It is presumed that the discussion upon the ordinance
while it was being amended, revealed the fact that the House
was "favorably disposed." But the question of how he discovered the fact, is of little moment compared with the fact
itself. No one can contemplate the harmonious adoption of
an anti-slavery measure under the conditions which then
existed, without asking the reason. The explanation is to
be found (1) in the constitution of Congress at the time, (2)
in the peculiar conditions caused by the application of the

¹ Bancroft, *Hist. of U. S.* (Fin. Rev.), vi., 285, and *Hist. of Formation of
Const.*, ii., 110.
² Above, Sec. V.

Ohio Company for a purchase of lands, and (3) in the political reasons which affected the southern members.

The Congress of the summer of 1787 was materially affected by the sessions of the Constitutional Convention. Many of the strong men of North and South were attending it at Philadelphia, and the Old Congress was left with a somewhat quiet and peaceable company of men. Its most efficient members were heartily in sympathy with the amendment in question, and naturally carried much influence with them. On the final vote the list showed but eighteen names, and among these there were none others such as Grayson, Carrington, and Lee. The Virginia triumvirate is worthy of note. They were the backbone and energy of the whole body: Grayson, temporary president:[1] Carrington, chairman of the two important committees; and R. H. Lee, the man whose arrival had so impressed Dane. The presence of the agent of the Ohio Company, who was on intimate terms with these men, had no small influence in enlisting their sympathies in the cause of the new settlement, and this must have extended perforce to the ordinance for its government. Grayson had exerted his influence on every occasion in behalf of the West, and now he had more reason than ever to do the same. The general effect of the prospective purchase of lands upon the finances of the government tended to put Congress in a good humor. To deal with the public debt had been the most difficult task of the Confederate Congress, and the prospect of immediate liquidation of a large share must have had a marked effect upon the action of every member of that body. The personal influence of Cutler, even though not exerted especially in behalf of the ordi-

---

[1] It appears that St. Clair did not arrive until all chance for his personal influence to affect the ordinance had passed. Gen. Irvine and Gen. St. Clair arrived "in time to take our seats" July 17, four days after the passage of the ordinance: Gen. Irvine to Gen. Butler, July 19, 1787 : *St. Clair Papers*, i., 604. A traditional view of Grayson's connection with the Ordinance of 1787 is preserved in the *Annals of Congress* for 1819, where he is said to have drawn the Ordinance: *Annals*, 15th Cong., 2d Sess., 1225. His influence as temporary president, and also chairman of the committee which framed the report, was very great.

nance, is not to be underrated in accounting for the unanimity of feeling among the members.

What reasons, however, would one of the southern members have given for favoring this measure ? Grayson himself mentions some and hints at others, in a letter to Monroe not long after.[1]   He says : " The clause respecting slavery was agreed to by southern members for the purpose of preventing tobacco and indigo being made on the north-west side of the Ohio, as well as for several other political reasons." How much effect the prospect of a monopoly of these two industries had upon the southern vote, it is impossible to tell : but it was perhaps only one of many reasons for their vote. The question of the navigation of the Mississippi was discussed long after 1787, and the present vote of the South has been regarded as a concession to the Northeast, in order to bring about a more favorable settlement of the Mississippi question.[2]   It is evident that the interests of the South would appear to be advanced in several ways : a settlement of the Northwest would make a greater demand for an open Mississippi ; it would ultimately prove a barrier against the Indians, and therefore give greater value to the lands south of the Ohio ; settlement along the north side of that river would tend to hold the settlements on the south side from Spanish connection.   The ultimate effect upon the Southwest might appear far from small, and the members from the South might, indeed, easily believe that the protected monopoly of the indigo and tobacco industries would soon people thickly the southwestern country and give them the political ascendancy over the North.[3]   The measure itself was not so obnoxious to southern men generally as it might otherwise be, since it was coupled with the fugitive-slave clause.   This, it has been noted, was added to the motion of King by a committee in 1785.[4]   It can hardly have done

[1] August 8, 1787 : Dunn, *Indiana*, 212 ; Stone, *Penn. Mag. of Hist. and Biog.*, xiii., 338.

[2] Stone, *Penn. Mag. of Hist. and Biog.*, xiii., 333.   *Cf.* above, Sec. VI. (b).

[3] *Cf.* on these questions, Dunn, *Indiana*, 210–4 ; Stone, *Ordinance of 1787*. in *Penn. Mag. of Hist. and Biog.*, xiii., 328–33.

[4] Above, Sec. V.

more than make the proposition less objectionable to members from slave States. It certainly could have offered no inducement to them to vote for the article. More than this, the language of Dane implies that whatever effect the combination of the prohibitory and fugitive clauses may have had upon the vote, it was accomplished without discussion.

This completed the formation of the Ordinance of 1787. The next day the third reading was had, and by the vote of every State present it became the first active constitution of the Northwest Territory.[1]

---

[1] The vote on the final passage was unanimous. But, as the voting was done by States, this means only that the vote of each State was affirmative. The vote of every member but one also favored the passage of the Ordinance. Yates of New York was much opposed to the measure and required the yeas and nays. The members present were as follows :

Massachusetts : Samuel Halter, Nathan Dane.

New York : Melancthon Smith, John Herring, Peter W. Yates. [^]

New Jersey : Abraham Clark, Mr. Schureman.

Delaware : Dyre Kearney, Nathaniel Mitchell.

Virginia : William Grayson, Richard H. Lee, Edward Carrington.

North Carolina : William Blount, Benjamin Hawkins.

South Carolina : John Kean, Daniel Huger.

Georgia : William Few, William Pierce.

Other States absent. NH. Myl. , R.I.

Force, *Hist. of Ordinance*, in *St. Clair Papers*, ii., 611, and *Life of Cutler*, ii., 417–8 ; Sparks, *Writings of Washington*, xii., 420–5 (for given names of members) ; Donaldson, *Public Domain*, 152 ; Bancroft, *Hist. of U. S.* (Fin. Rev.), vi., 289–90, and *Hist. of Formation of Const.*, ii., 115–6.

XI.

BIBLIOGRAPHY OF THE TEXT OF THE ORDINANCE.

Poore, *Charters*, 429-32 ; Chase, *Statutes of Ohio and Northwest Territory*, i., 66-9 ; *U. S. Statutes at Large*, i., 51-3 ; Porter, *Outlines of U. S. Constitution*, 63-9 ; Donaldson, *Public Domain*, 153-6 ; Dillon, *Hist. of Indiana*, 597-601 ; Albach, *Western Annals*, 466-72 ; Force, *Hist. of Ordinance : St. Clair Papers*, ii., 612-18, and *Life of Cutler*, ii., 419-27 ; *Journals of Congress*, iv., 752, cited by Winsor, *Narr. and Crit. Hist. of Amer.*, vii., 538 ; *Mag. of West. Hist.*, i., 56-9 ; Cooper, *American Politics*, iv., 10-13 ; I. W. Andrews, *Manual of Const. of U. S.*, App., xiii.-xix.; Perkins, *Western Annals*, 293-8 ; Merriam, *Hist. of Ordinance*, 24-35 ; *Penn. Archives*, xi., 162-8.

The text is also found in most editions of the statutes and laws of Ohio, Indiana, Illinois, Michigan, Wisconsin, and Minnesota, especially the earlier ones. *Cf.* the following :—OHIO : *Land Laws for Ohio* (1825), 252-8 ; Chase's *Statutes* (above) ; *Statutes* (1841), 42-49 ; *Public Statutes at Large* (1853-61), i., 86-92 ; *Rev. Statutes* (1880), i., 46-50 ; Williams, *Rev. Statutes* ii., 1686-90 ; *Verified Rev. Statutes* (1890), 3174-8. INDIANA : *Rev. Laws* (1824), 23-9 ; *Rev. Laws* (1831), 24-9 ; *Rev. Laws* (1838), 23-8 ; *Rev. Laws* (1852), i., 77-84 ; *Rev. Statutes* (1888), ii., App. ILLINOIS : *State Digest*, *1810-81*, iii., 2028-9 ; *Rev. Statutes* (1845), 11-15 ; *Statutes* (1858), 20-5 ; *Statutes, 1818-69*, 7-10 ; *Rev. Statutes* (1884), 20-24 ; *Annotated Statutes* (1885), i., 42-6. MICHIGAN : *Rev. Statutes* (1838), 24-9 ; *Rev. Statutes* (1846), 739-44 ; *Compiled Laws* (1857), i., 23-30 ; *Compiled Laws* (1872), i., 25-32 ; WISCONSIN : *Statutes* (1839), 14-19 ; *Rev. Statutes* (1849), 773-8 ; *Rev. Statutes* (1858), 1065-71 ; *Rev. Statutes* (1871), i., 61-7. MINNESOTA : *Rev. Statutes of the Territory* (1851), 16-20 ; *Public Statutes* (1859), xiii.-xviii.

THE ORDINANCE OF 1787.

An Ordinance for the Government of the Territory of the United States Northwest of the River Ohio.

Be it ordained by the United States, in Congress assembled, That the said Territory, for the purposes of temporary government, be one district ; subject, however, to be divided into two districts, as future circumstances may, in the opinion of Congress, make it expedient.

Be it ordained by the authority aforesaid, That the estates both of resident and non-resident proprietors in the said Territory, dying intestate, shall descend to and be distributed among their children and the descendants of a deceased child in equal parts; the descendants of a deceased

I.—THE LAW OF DESCENT AND CONVEYANCE OF ESTATES. child or grandchild to take the share of their deceased parent in equal parts among them; and where there shall be no children or descendants, then in equal parts to the next of kin, in equal degree; and among collaterals, the children of a deceased brother or sister of the intestate shall have in equal parts among them their deceased parent's share; and there shall in no case be a distinction between kindred of the whole and half-blood; saving in all cases to the widow of the intestate her third part of the real estate for life, and one third part of the personal estate; and this law relative to descents and dower shall remain in full force until altered by the legislature of the district. And until the governor and judges shall adopt laws as hereinafter mentioned, estates in the said Territory may be devised or bequeathed by wills in writing signed and sealed by him or her in whom the estate may be (being of full age) and attested by three witnesses; and real estates may be conveyed by lease and release, or bargain and sale, signed, sealed, and delivered by the person, being of full age, in whom the estate may be, and attested by two witnesses, provided such wills be duly proved, and such conveyances be acknowledged, or the execution of thereof duly proved, and be recorded within one year after a proper magistrate, courts, and registers, shall be appointed for that purpose; and personal property may be transferred by delivery, saving, however, to the French and Canadian inhabitants, and other settlers of Kaskaskias, St. Vincents, and the neighboring villages, who have heretofore professed themselves citizens of Virginia, their laws and customs now in force among them relative to the descent and conveyance of property.

Be it ordained by the authority aforesaid, That there shall
be appointed, from time to time, by Congress, a governor,
whose commission shall continue in force for the term of
II.—THE TER- three years, unless sooner revoked by Congress :
RITORIAL he shall reside in the district and have a free-
GOVERNMENT. hold estate therein, in one thousand acres of
land, while in the exercise of his office.

There shall be appointed, from time to time, by Congress,
a secretary, whose commission shall continue in force for
four years, unless sooner revoked : he shall reside in the
district, and have a freehold estate therein, in five hundred
acres of land, while in the exercise of his office. It shall be
his duty to keep and preserve the acts and laws passed by
the legislature, and the public records of the district, of the
proceedings of the governor in his executive department,
and transmit authentic copies of such acts and proceedings
every six months to the Secretary of Congress.

There shall also be appointed a court, to consist of three
judges, any two of whom to form a court, who shall have a
common-law jurisdiction, and reside in the district, and have
each therein a freehold estate, in five hundred acres of land,
while in the exercise of their offices ; and their commissions
shall continue in force during good behavior.

The governor and judges, or a majority of them, shall
adopt and publish in the district such laws of the original
States, criminal and civil, as may be necessary and best suited
to the circumstances of the district, and report them to Congress from time to time, which laws shall be in force in the
district until the organization of the General Assembly
therein, unless disapproved of by Congress ; but afterwards
the legislature shall have authority to alter them as they
shall think fit. The governor for the time being, shall be
commander-in-chief of the militia, and appoint and commission all officers in the same below the rank of general officers ;
all general officers shall be appointed and commissioned by
Congress.

Previous to the organization of the General Assembly, the
governor shall appoint such magistrates in each county or town-

ship as he shall find necessary for the preservation of the
peace and good order in the same. After the General Assembly shall be organized, the powers and duties of magistrates
and other civil officers shall be regulated and defined by the
said Assembly; but all magistrates and other civil officers,
not herein otherwise directed, shall, during the continuance
of this temporary government, be appointed by the governor.

For the prevention of crimes and injuries, the laws to
be adopted or made shall have force in all parts of the
district, and for the execution of process, criminal and civil,
the governor shall make proper divisions thereof ; and he
shall proceed, from time to time, as circumstances may
require, to lay out the parts of the district in which the
Indian title shall have been extinguished, into counties and
townships, subject, however, to such alterations as may
thereafter be made by the legislature.

So soon as there shall be five thousand free male inhabitants, of full age, in the district, upon giving proof thereof
to the governor, they shall receive authority, with time and
place, to elect representatives from their counties or townships, to represent them in the General Assembly : *provided,*
that, for every five hundred free male inhabitants, there shall
be one representative, and so on progressively with the number of free male inhabitants shall the right of representation
increase, until the number of representatives shall amount
to twenty-five ; after which the number and proportion of
representatives shall be regulated by the legislature : *provided,* that no person shall be eligible or qualified to act as a
representative, unless he shall have been a citizen of one of
the United States three years, and be a resident in the
district, or unless he shall have resided in the district three
years, and, in either case, he shall likewise hold in his own
right, in fee simple, two hundred acres of land within the
same : *provided, also,* that a freehold in fifty acres of land
in the district, having been a citizen of one of the States, and
being resident in the district, or the like freehold and two
years' residence in the district, shall be necessary to qualify
a man as an elector of a representative.

The representatives thus elected shall serve for the term of two years: and, in the case of the death of the representative, or removal from office, the governor shall issue a writ to the county or township for which he was a member, to elect another in his stead, to serve for the residue of the term.

The General Assembly, or legislature, shall consist of a governor, legislative council, and a House of Representatives. The legislative council shall consist of five members to continue in office five years, unless sooner removed by Congress, any three of whom to be a quorum, and the members of the council shall be nominated and appointed in the following manner, to wit: As soon as representatives shall be elected, the governor shall appoint a time and place for them to meet together, and, when met, they shall nominate ten persons, residents of the district, and each possessed of a freehold in five hundred acres of land, and return their names to Congress; five of whom Congress shall appoint and commission as aforesaid; and whenever a vacancy shall happen in the council, by death or removal from office, the House of Representatives shall nominate two persons, qualified as aforesaid, for each vacancy, and return their names to Congress; one of whom Congress shall appoint and commission for the residue of the term; and every five years, four months at least before the expiration of the time of service of the members of the council, the said House shall nominate ten persons, qualified as aforesaid, and return their names to Congress, five of whom Congress shall appoint and commission to serve as members of the council five years unless sooner removed. And the governor, legislative council, and House of Representatives, shall have authority to make laws in all cases, for the good government of the district, not repugnant to the principles and articles in this ordinance established and declared. And all bills having passed by a majority in the House, and by a majority in the council, shall be referred to the governor for his assent; but no bill or legislative act whatever shall be of any force without his assent. The governor shall have power to convene, prorogue, and dissolve the General Assembly, when, in his opinion, it shall be expedient.

The governor, judges, legislative council, secretary, and other such officers as Congress shall appoint in the district, shall take an oath or affirmation of fidelity and of office ; the governor before the president of Congress, and all other officers before the governor. As soon as a legislature shall be formed in the district, the council and House, assembled in one room, shall have authority by joint ballot to elect a delegate to Congress, who shall have a seat in Congress, with a right of debating, but not of voting, during this temporary government.

And for extending the fundamental principles of civil and religious liberty, which form the basis whereon these republics, their laws, and constitutions are erected ; to fix and establish those principles as the basis of all laws, constitutions, and governments which shall hereafter be formed in the said territory ; to provide also for the establishment of States, and permanent government therein, and for their admission to a share in the Federal councils, on an equal footing with the original States, at as early periods as may be consistent with the general interest.

III.—THE ARTI-CLES OF COM-PACT.

It is hereby ordained and declared by the authority aforesaid, That the following articles shall be considered as articles of compact between the original States and the people and States in the said territory, and forever remain unalterable, unless by common consent, to-wit :

ARTICLE I.   No person demeaning himself in a peaceable and orderly manner shall ever be molested on account of his mode of worship or religious sentiments in the said territory.

ARTICLE II.   The inhabitants of the said territory shall always be entitled to the benefits of the writ of *habeas corpus* and of trial by jury ; of a proportionate representation of the people in the legislature, and of judicial proceedings according to the course of the common law ; all persons shall be bailable, unless for capital offenses, where the proof shall be evident or the presumption great ; all fines shall be moderate, and no cruel or unusual punishments shall be inflicted; no man shall be deprived of his liberty or property but by the judgment of his peers, or the law of the land ; and should the public exigencies make it necessary, for the common preservation, to take any person's property, or to demand his particular services, full compensation shall be made for the same ; and, in the just preservation of rights and property, it is understood and declared that no law ought ever to be made, or have force in the said territory, that shall, in any manner whatever, interfere with or affect private contracts or engagements bona fide and without fraud, previously formed.

ARTICLE III. Religion, morality, and knowledge, being necessary to good government and the happiness of mankind, schools and the means of education shall forever be encouraged. The utmost good faith shall always be observed toward the Indians; their lands and property shall never be taken from them without their consent ; and, in their property, rights, and liberty, they never shall be invaded or disturbed, unless in just and lawful wars authorized by Congress ; but laws founded in justice and humanity shall, from time to time, be made, for preventing wrongs being done to them and for preserving peace and friendship with them.

ARTICLE IV. The said territory and the States which may be formed therein, shall forever remain a part of this Confederacy of the United States of America, subject to the Articles of Confederation and to such alterations therein as shall constitutionally be made ; and to all the acts and ordinances of the United States, in Congress assembled, conformable thereto. The inhabitants and settlers in the said territory shall be subject to pay a part of the Federal debts, contracted or to be contracted, and a proportional part of the expenses of government, to be apportioned on them by Congress, according to the same common rule and measure by which apportionments thereof shall be made on the other States ; and the taxes for paying their proportion shall be laid and levied by the authority and direction of the legislatures of the district or districts, or new States, as in the original States, within the time agreed upon by the United States, in Congress assembled. The legislatures of those districts, or new States, shall never interfere with the primary disposal of the soil by the United States, in Congress assembled, nor with any regulations Congress may find necessary for securing the title in such soil to the bona fide purchasers. No tax shall be imposed on lands the property of the United States; and in no case shall non-resident proprietors be taxed higher than residents. The navigable waters leading into the Mississippi and St. Lawrence, and the carrying-places between the same, shall be common highways and forever free, as well to the inhabitants of the said territory as to the citizens of the United States, and those of any other States that may be admitted into the Confederacy, without any tax impost, or duty therefor.

ARTICLE V. There shall be formed in the said territory not less than three nor more than five States; and the boundaries of the States, as soon as Virginia shall alter her act of cession and consent to the same, shall become fixed and established as follows, to-wit: The western State in the said territory shall be bounded by the Mississippi, the Ohio, and Wabash Rivers; a direct line drawn from the Wabash and Post Vincent's due north to the territorial line between the United States and Canada, and by the said territorial line to the Lake of the Woods and Mississippi. The middle State shall be bounded by the said direct line, the Wabash from Post Vincent's to the Ohio; by the Ohio, by a direct line drawn due north from the mouth of the Great Miami to the said territorial line and by the said territorial line. The eastern State shall be bounded by the last-mentioned direct line, the Ohio, Pennsylvania, and the said territorial line, *Provided*, however, and it is further understood and declared, that the boundaries of these three States shall be subject so far to be altered, that if Congress shall hereafter find it expedient, they shall have authority to form one or two States in that part of the said territory which lies north of an east and west line drawn through the southerly bend or extreme of Lake Michigan; and whenever any of the said States shall have sixty thousand free inhabitants therein, such State shall be admitted by its delegates into the Congress of the United States on an equal footing with the original States, in all respects whatever; and shall be at liberty to form a permanent constitution and State government; *Provided*, the constitution so to be formed shall be republican and in conformity to the principles contained in these articles; and, so far as it can be consistent with the general interest of the Confederacy, such admissions shall be allowed at an earlier period, and when there may be a less number of free inhabitants in the States than sixty thousand.

ARTICLE VI.   There shall be neither slavery nor involuntary servitude in the said territory, otherwise than in punishment of crimes whereof the party shall have been duly convicted; *Provided*, always, that any person escaping into the same, from whom labor or service is lawfully claimed in any one of the original States, such fugitive may be lawfully reclaimed and conveyed to the person claiming his or her labor or service as aforesaid.

Be it ordained by the authority aforesaid, That the .resolutions of the 23d of April, 1784, relative to the subject of this ordinance, be and the same are hereby repealed and declared null and void.

Done by the United States in Congress assembled, on the 13th day of July, in the year of our Lord 1787, and of their sovereignty and independence the 12th.

CHAS. THOMSON, Sec'y.

AUTHORITIES.

— ADAMS, H. B.   Maryland's Influence upon Land Cessions to the United States.   In J. II. U. Studies, Third Series, i.   Baltimore, 1885.

ALBACH, J. R.   Annals of the West.   Pittsburg, 1857.

ANDREWS, I. W.   The Beginnings of the Colonial System of the United States : *Ohio Archæological and Historical Quarterly*, i.   The Northwest Territory : *Magazine of American History*, xv., August, 1886.

ANDREWS, I. W.   Manual of the Constitution of the United States.   Cincinnati and New York.

ANNALS OF CONGRESS, 1789-1824.   Gales and Seaton edition.   Washington, 1834-56.

ARNOLD, S. G. History of the State of Rhode Island. 2 vols. New York, 1874.

ATWATER, CALEB. History of the State of Ohio. Cincinnati.

BANCROFT, GEORGE. ⟋ History of the Formation of the Constitution. 2 vols. New York, 1883.

BANCROFT, GEORGE. History of the United States of America, from the Discovery of the Continent. 6 vols. New York, 1888.

BENTON, T. H. Abridgment of the Debates of Congress, from 1789 to 1856. 16 vols. New York, 1860–61.

BRYANT, W. C., and GAY, S. H. A Popular History of the United States. 4 vols. New York.

BURNET, JACOB. Notes on the Early Settlement of the Northwestern Territory. Cincinnati, 1847.

CAMPBELL, J. V. Outlines of the Political History of Michigan. Detroit, 1876.

CARPENTER, W. H., and ARTHUR, T. S. The History of Illinois. Philadelphia, 1857.

CARR, LUCIEN. Missouri. Commonwealth Series. Boston and New York, 1888.

CHASE, S. P. The Statutes of Ohio and the Northwestern Territory. Cincinnati, 1833–35.

COOLEY, THOMAS. Michigan. Commonwealth Series. Boston, 1885. Compiled Laws of Michigan (see under " Michigan ").

COOPER and FENTON. American Politics. Philadelphia, 1882 ; also Chicago.

COX, S. S. Three Decades of Federal Legislation. Providence, 1885.

CRICHFIELD, L. J. (See under " Ohio," *Reports of Supreme Court.*)

CURTIS, G. T. History of the Origin, Formation, and Adoption of the Constitution of the United States. 2 vols. New York, 1865.

CUTLER, W. P., and JULIA P. Life, Journals, and Correspondence of Rev. Manasseh Cutler, LL.D. 2 vols. Cincinnati, 1888.

CUTLER, W. P. Private Contract Provision in the Ordinance of 1787 : *Magazine of American History*, xxii. The Ordinance of July 13th, 1787 : *Ohio Archæological and Historical Quarterly*, i., 1887.

DANE, NATHAN. General Abridgment and Digest of American Laws, ix., Appendix : King's *Ohio*, App. ii. Letter to Rufus King, July 16, 1787 : Bancroft, *Hist. of Formation of Const.*, ii., App. and elsewhere. Letter to Daniel Webster, March 26, 1830 : *Mass. Hist. Soc. Proc., 1867–1869.* Letter to J. H. Farnham, May 12, 1831 : Merriam, *Hist. of Ordinance*, 37.

DAVIDSON, A., and STUVE, B. A Complete History of Illinois, 1673–1884. Springfield, 1884.

DILLON, J. B. A History of Indiana. Indianapolis, 1859.

DONALDSON, THOMAS. The Public Domain. Its History with Statistics. House Miscellaneous, 2d Sess., 47th Cong., 1882–83, vol. xix. Washington, 1884.

DUNN, J. P., Jr. Indiana. Commonwealth Series. Boston and New York, 1888.

EDWARDS, N. W. History of Illinois from 1778 to 1833, and Life and Times of Ninian Edwards. Springfield, 1870.

ELIOT, SAMUEL. Manual of United States History. Boston, 1856.

ELLIOT, JONATHAN. Debates on the Adoption of the Federal Constitution. 5 vols. Philadelphia, 1876.

FARMER, SILAS. History of Detroit and Michigan. Detroit, 1884.

FISKE, JOHN. Critical Period of American History. Boston and New York, 1888.

FISKE, JOHN. Civil Government in the United States, Considered with some Reference to its Origins. Boston and New York, 1890.

FORCE, PETER. American Archives, Fifth Series, vol. iii. Washington, 1853.

FORD, THOMAS. A History of Illinois. Chicago, 1854.

GANET, HENRY. Boundaries of the United States : Bulletin of the United States Geographical Survey, No. 13. Washington, 1885.

GILMAN, D. C. James Monroe. Statesmen Series. Boston, 1885.

GOODELL, WILLIAM. Slavery and Anti-Slavery. New York, 1853.

HENING, W. W. The Statutes at Large : being a Collection of all the Laws of Virginia from the First Session of the Legislature, in the Year 1619. 13 vols. Richmond (vols. 1-12) and Philadelphia (vol. 13), 1809-1823.

HAMILTON, J. C. Works of Alexander Hamilton. 7 vols. New York, 1851.

HAMILTON, J. C. History of the Republic of the United States of America, as traced in the Writings of Alexander Hamilton. 2 vols. New York, 1857–58.

HILDRETH, RICHARD. The History of the United States of America. 6 vols. 1880–82.

HINSDALE, B. A. The Old Northwest. New York, 1888.

HOLST, HERMANN VON. Constitutional History of the United States, 1750–1832. Translated by J. J. Lalor and A. B. Mason. Chicago, 1876.

HOWARD, G. E. An Introduction to the Local Constitutional History of the United States. Vol. i. Baltimore, 1889.

HOWE, D. W. The Laws and Courts of Northwest and Indiana Territories : Indiana Historical Society Pamphlets, No. 1. Indianapolis, 1886.

ILLINOIS. Illinois State Digest, 1810–81, 6 vols., edited by E. J. Hill ; Chicago, 1879–87. Revised Statutes, edited by M. Brayman, Springfield, 1845 ; Statutes of Illinois, edited by Scates, Treat and Blackwell, Chicago, 1858 ; Statutes of Illinois, 1818–69, edited by E. L. Gross, Springfield, 1872 ; Revised Statutes of the State of Illinois, 1884, edited by H. B. Hurd, Springfield, 1874 ; Annotated Statutes of the State of Illinois, edited by Starr and Curtis, 2 vols., Chicago, 1885.

INDIANA. The Revised Laws of Indiana, Corydon, 1824 ; Revised Statutes, Indianapolis, 1831 ; Revised Statutes, Indianapolis, 1838 ; Revised Statutes, 2 vols., Indianapolis, 1852 ; Revised Statutes, Chicago, 1883.

JOHNSTON, ALEXANDER. Ordinance of 1787, and Territories. In Lalor's Cyclopædia of Political Science (1884).

JOHNSTON, ALEXANDER. The United States, its History and Constitution. New York, 1889.

KING, RUFUS. Ohio. Commonwealth Series. Boston and New York, 1888.

KNIGHT, G. W. History and Management of Land Grants for Education in the Northwest Territory. Papers of the American Historical Association, i., No. 3. New York and London, 1885.

LALOR, J. J. Cyclopædia of Political Science, Political Economy, and Political History of the United States. 3 vols. Chicago, 1882–84.

LANDON, J. S. Constitutional History and Government of the United States. Boston and New York, 1889.

LANMAN, J. H. History of Michigan. New York, 1855.

LIBRARY OF UNIVERSAL KNOWLEDGE. Reprint of 1880 edition of Chambers's Encyclopædia. New York, 1881.

LINN, WILLIAM. Life of Thomas Jefferson. Ithaca, 1843.

MADISON, JAMES. Letters and Other Writings of James Madison. 4 vols. Philadelphia, 1865. Reports of the Federal Convention : Elliot's Debates, v.

MAGAZINE OF AMERICAN HISTORY. 23 vols. Edited by Martha J. Lamb. New York, 1877–90.

MAGAZINE OF WESTERN HISTORY. 11 vols. Cleveland and New York, 1884–90.

MASSACHUSETTS. Acts and Resolves of the Province of Massachusetts Bay, edited by Ellis Ames and A. C. Goodell, 5 vols., Boston, 1869–86. The Laws of the Commonwealth of Massachusetts, 1780–1801, 3 vols., Boston, 1807.

McMASTER, J. B. A History of the People of the United States. 2 vols. New York, 1885.

MERRIAM, J. M. The Legislative History of the Ordinance of 1787. Worcester, Mass., 1888.

MICHIGAN. Pioneer and Historical Collections, 14 vols., Lansing, 1877–90 ; The Revised Statutes of the State of Michigan, edited by E. B. Harrington and E. J. Roberts, Detroit, 1838 ; Revised Statutes of the State, edited by S. M. Green, Detroit, 1846; The Compiled Laws of the State, edited by T. M. Cooley, 2 vols., Lansing, 1857 ; The Compiled Laws, edited by J. S. Dewey, 2 vols., Lansing, 1872.

MINNESOTA. Revised Statutes of the Territory of Minnesota, edited by M. S. Wilkinson, St. Paul, 1851 ; The Public Statutes of the State, edited by M. Sherburne and W. Hollinshead, St. Paul, 1859.

MONETTE, J. W. History of the Discovery and Settlement of the Valley of the Mississippi. 2 vols. New York, 1848.

MOSES, JOHN. Illinois. Historical and Statistical, Comprising the Essential Facts of its Planting and Growth as a Province, County, Territory, and State. Vol. i. Chicago, 1889.

NORTH AMERICAN REVIEW, vols. liii. and cxxii. Boston, 1841, 1876.

OHIO ARCHÆOLOGICAL AND HISTORICAL QUARTERLY. 2 vols. Columbus.

OHIO. Land Laws for Ohio : A Compilation of Laws, Treaties, Resolutions, and Ordinances of the General and State Governments which Relate to Lands in the State of Ohio, including the Laws Adopted by the Governor and Judges, the Laws of the Territorial Legislature, and the Laws of this State, to the Years 1815–16, Columbus, 1825. The Statutes of Ohio and Northwest Territory (see under " Chase ") ; The Statutes of the State of Ohio, Columbus, 1841 ; Public Statutes at Large, edited by M. E. Curwen, 4 vols., Cincinnati, 1853–61 ; Revised Statutes of the State, edited by J. M. Williams, 3 vols., Cincinnati, 1886 ; The Verified Revised Statutes of the State, edited by R. B.

Smith and A. B. Benedict, 2 vols, Cincinnati, 1890 ; Reports of the Supreme Court of Ohio, New Series, ix., Columbus, 1860.

PERKINS, J. H. Annals of the West. Cincinnati, 1847.

PICKERING, OCTAVIUS. The Life of Timothy Pickering. Vol. i. Boston, 1867.

PITKIN, TIMOTHY. Political and Civil History of the United States of America. 2 vols. New Haven, 1828.

POOLE, W. F. Dr. Cutler and the Ordinance of 1787, *North Am. Rev.*, vol. cxxii., April, 1876. General Arthur St. Clair, Chicago *Dial*, ii. General St. Clair and the Ordinance of 1787, *ibid.*, iii.

POORE, BEN: PERLEY. Federal and State Constitutions, Colonial Charters, and Other Organic Laws of the United States. 2 vols. Washington, 1877.

PORTER, L. H. Outlines of Constitutional History of the United States. New York, 1883.

RANDALL, H. S. The Life of Thomas Jefferson. 3 vols. New York, 1858.

RIDPATH, J. C. Popular History of the United States of America. New York, 1889.

REPORT of the Commissioners of the National Centennial Celebration of the Early Settlement of the Territory Northwest of the River Ohio. Columbus, 1889.

SATO, SHOSUKE. History of the Land Question in the United States. In J. H. U. Studies, Fourth Series, vii.–ix. 1886.

SCHUCKERS, J. W. Life and Public Services of Salmon Portland Chase. New York, 1874.

SMITH, W. H. General St. Clair and the Ordinance of 1787, Chicago *Dial*, ii. The St. Clair Papers. 2 vols. Cincinnati, 1882.

SPARKS, JARED. Writings of George Washington. 12 vols. New York, 1847–48.

SPENCER, J. A. History of the United States from the Earliest Period to the Administration of James Madison. 3 vols. New York, 1857.

STAPLES, W. R. Rhode Island in the Continental Congress, 1765–1790. Providence, 1870.

STONE, F. D. The Ordinance of 1787, *Penn. Mag. of Hist. and Biog.*, xiii.

STRONG, M. M. History of the Territory of Wisconsin, 1836–1848. Madison, 1885.

TAYLOR, J. W. History of the State of Ohio, First Period, 1650–1787. Cincinnati, 1854.

UNITED STATES STATUTES AT LARGE. Vol. i. Boston, 1850.

VIRGINIA. Calendar of Virginia State Papers and Other Manuscripts. Edited by Palmer, McRae, and Calston. 7 vols. 1875–88.

WALKER, C. M. History of Athens County, Ohio. Cincinnati, 1869.

WASHINGTON, H. A. The Writings of Jefferson. Vols. ii.–ix. Washington, 1853–54 ; also New York, 1884.

WEBSTER, DANIEL, Works of. 6 vols. Boston, 1877.

WESTERN RESERVE HISTORICAL SOCIETY PUBLICATIONS, vol. ii. Tracts 37–42. Cleveland, 1888.

WHITTLESEY, CHARLES. Miscellaneous Papers. Cleveland, 1886.

—— WILLIAMS, W. W.   Arthur St. Clair and the Ordinance of 1787, *Mag. of Western Hist.*, i.

WINSOR, JUSTIN.   Narrative and Critical History of America.   8 vols.   Boston and New York, 1886–89.

WISCONSIN.   Statutes of the Territory, Albany, 1839 ; The Revised Statutes of the State, Southport, 1849 ; The Revised Statutes of the State, Chicago, 1858 ; Revised Statutes of the State, edited by David Taylor, 2 vols., St. Louis, 1871.

www.ingramcontent.com/pod-product-compliance
Lightning Source LLC
Chambersburg PA
CBHW030541270326
41927CB00008B/1461